BUT IF YOU'RE
GOING TO BE THE

MOST

EXPENSIVE
YOU HAVE TO BE

THE BEST

'Andrew Griffiths has a unique gift. He is one of the greatest communicators of our time. Part philosopher, part futurist and part advocate for entrepreneurs everywhere.'

Shelley Wild, CEO, PeopleHQ and Founder of *the* Human Learning Collective www.humanlearningcollective.com.au

'Anyone can be the cheapest, the art is being a brand and service that is highly valued. In Andrew's new book he takes you on a journey that makes you think bigger, bolder and braver than ever before to create an offering that is memorable, referable and loveable. This book is a total game changer!'

Keith Abraham, Multi-Award Winning Global Speaker, Five-Times Best Selling Author www.keithabraham.com

'Andrew Griffiths is real, raw and relevant.'

The Sunday Mail

'Andrew Griffiths is the eighth wonder of the world. He embodies authority, integrity and authenticity when it comes to doing business, and the success of the people he works with is mirrored around the planet. Those of us in his community are loyal, grateful and fiercely willing to support his extraordinary entrepreneurial work.'

Darren Finkelstein, The Accountability Coach, Author and Mentor www.tickthoseboxes.com.au

'There is no one else like Andrew Griffiths. He's larger than life, totally driven to help others, and he makes doing business a blast.'

Anh Doh, Comedian, Author and Speaker

'Andrew Griffiths – we salute you.'

Weekend Sunrise

'Andrew Griffiths is one of the best authorities I know on how to do business better. He is a never-ending source of smart information and powerful inspiration.'

Brian Haverty, Formerly Editorial Content Manager, CBS Interactive

'I've been fortunate enough to work and collaborate with Andrew over the past four years and I have deeply valued his integrity, honesty and deep insight. Through his carefully considered counsel, my business has flourished.'

Katrina McCarter, CEO, Marketing to Mums and OUT LOUD Marketing Partnerships www.katrinamccarter.com

'It is no wonder that the top business people in 65 countries read and apply his material. Quite simply, the value he provides is immense.'

Blake Beattie, Author, BULLSEYE and Founder of Pay It Forward Day

'In my dealings with Andrew I am constantly impressed by his generosity of spirit, humility and kindness, let alone his extraordinary entrepreneurial firepower.'

Geoff Anderson, Author, Speaker, Founder Sonic Sight www.sonicsight.com.au

'You know what I like most about Andrew Griffiths? His energy, enthusiasm and ability to see the best in something (business and life). Add to that a depth of business knowledge that is simply incredible and you get someone who knows their stuff and can deliver it in a way that people just get. That brings out the best in all of us.'

Rowdy McLean MBA, FAIM, CSP, 2019 Keynote Speaker of the Year www.rowdymclean.com

'Priceless! He's done it again. Andrew unearths value everywhere and shows us how to package it perfectly.'

Robert Gerrish, Solo Business Advocate www.robertgerrish.com

'Andrew Griffiths is simply one of a kind. He has a generous and warm heart that nurtures people to achieve more than they ever imagined was possible. He has lived a huge life and is willing to share the good, the bad and the ugly to help others grow (or just feel better about themselves!).'

Bree James, Author, Speaker and Entrepreneur www.breejames.com.au

'When I think about people who really understand entrepreneurs and business owners, there are a unique few that stand out around the world; Andrew Griffiths is one of them. Not only does he know the ins and outs of building a truly successful business, but he has the biggest heart and he is beyond generous in being able to help his clients create the shift they're looking for.'

Jane Anderson, Voted #3 Branding Expert Globally, Certified Speaker, Author of seven books including *Catalyst Content*
www.janeandersonspeaks.com

'Andrew Griffiths brings his full authentic personality and decades of rich experience to everything he does, building a high degree of credibility and trust in his advice, wrapped up in an easygoing style that helps you relax and engage with what he shares.'

Robert Nankervis, Leadership Advisor, Scaling Up Certified Coach, Speaker and Author www.robertnankervis.com

'Andrew Griffiths is a very unique human being. He is one of those very rare souls that you only meet once or twice in your life who really cares about everyone around him, who gives and keeps on giving selflessly without ever expecting anything in return. And behind his fun-loving, self-deprecating wit is a sharp mind, a warm wisdom and attention to detail that creates powerful insights and incredible bolts of inspirational magic, time and time again.'

Bushy Martin, *Get Invested* Author and Podcast Host
www.knowhowproperty.com.au

'After an intensive and challenging three-week tour of England, with a wide range of varied events throughout the country, the audience net promoter average across Andrew's events was 9.7/10 – it was, without a doubt, the highest of any presenter we had ever had. A truly extraordinary result from a truly extraordinary speaker and authority.'

Luke Renehan, Head of Marketing and Events, Newable
www.newable.co.uk

Other titles by Andrew Griffiths

It was a cold, wet and miserable morning ...

How on earth did I find myself standing on a deserted street, outside a nondescript, weather-beaten and kind of derelict-looking building on a wet and wild winter morning in Melbourne, basically waiting to score? I looked around tentatively and walked up to the blacked-out window, knocked three times, took a step back and waited.

After what felt like an eternity the window opened and a serious-looking hipster dude asked me what I wanted. I said, 'I'm here to pick up my … order.' I shoved my phone with the instructions that had been emailed to me in his face, a little too desperately. He looked at it, then he looked me up and down slowly, mumbling something under his breath. He turned abruptly and walked off.

I wasn't really sure what I had to do now. Should I just get in my car and make a run for it? Or do I stand there and do my utmost to look cool, calm and confident? While deliberating on my next course of action the dude came back, with a very ordinary-looking brown paper bag – he handed it to me as if it were something precious, which of course it was. The bag felt much lighter than I imagined, and as I looked inside, he said, with a conspiratorial wink, 'You're all set for a very good weekend now', and he slammed the window shut.

I bolted for my car as the drizzle got heavier and climbed inside, turned on the heat and got mentally prepared to inspect my purchase. I opened the bag and took out one of two boxes nestled inside. I opened it gently and found, to my absolute delight, six puffy and light pieces of pure heaven, that were in fact crumpets. I had just scored my first Holy Crumpets, which is the name of the hipster brand responsible for these little mounds of love.

Were they magnificent? Oh, you had better believe it. Were they the best crumpets I'd ever eaten in my fifty-four years on this planet? Without a moment's doubt.

Now scoring these crumpets from a hole in the wall that is only open for three hours on a Saturday morning is just part of this process. I had to order them online, and they sell out within an hour or two of being made available. It has taken weeks just to get an order in. And I had to pay $28 for twelve crumpets, where the going price for crumpets at most grocery stores is $2 for six. So $4 for twelve from the bigger grocery stores versus $28 from Holy Crumpets.

So, let me get this straight: they have a ridiculous ordering process that requires you to pounce online the minute they go on sale (and you never know when that will be). You pay seven hundred percent more than the crumpets you can buy anywhere else, at your convenience, twenty-four hours a day. You have to go to a grungy part of town, risking life and limb to actually pick them up. And yet they sell out every single week and people rave about them.

All common sense would say that surely this can't work? Their business model is terrible, right? But is it? Someone has to be the most expensive, they most certainly are, but if you're going to be the most expensive, you have to be the best, and when it comes to crumpets these guys most certainly are.

This experience resonated deeply with me as I was in the midst of writing this book and it reinforced to me that there is an alternative business model to the hustle and the grind. There is a model that shows if you are absolutely prepared to do what it takes to be the very best at what you do, there are always going to be people who are prepared to find you and pay for what it is you are selling.

Imagine a business model where you are actually in control of your business. Let's be honest; in business most of us have a tiger by the tail where we just stagger from one day to the next and hang on for dear life. Imagine a business where you could earn what you deserve to earn, on your terms, where you can take pride in knowing that what you do is considered world-class in every way, and your customers know it and they are prepared to do whatever it takes to get a hold of your products or service. *You* drive this business. But it doesn't work without one key ingredient.

The key is being the best. That's not something that comes easily. Few people are really prepared to do what it takes. Those that are, get rewarded with a business that works for them. One built on value, integrity, commitment – a business of substance. And that's what I'm all about, working with people of substance to build businesses of substance. Holy Crumpets are my new heroes, and while their business model might not work for some, it's mighty appealing to those of us who are sick and tired of the alternative.

So this is the story I want you to consider as we begin our little journey together down the 'Someone has to be the most expensive, why not make it you?' road. Buckle in, it's going to be one seriously interesting and challenging ride, with a giant pay-off if you're brave enough to go the distance.

Andrew Griffiths

it takes to get a hold of your products or service. *You* drive this business. But it doesn't work without one key ingredient.

The key is being the best. That's not something that comes easily. Few people are really prepared to do what it takes. Those that are, get rewarded with a business that works for them. One built on value, integrity, commitment – a business of substance. And that's what I'm all about, working with people of substance to build businesses of substance. Holy Crumpets are my new heroes, and while their business model might not work for some, it's mighty appealing to those of us who are sick and tired of the alternative.

So this is the story I want you to consider as we begin our little journey together down the 'Someone has to be the most expensive, why not make it you?' road. Buckle in, it's going to be one seriously interesting and challenging ride, with a giant pay-off if you're brave enough to go the distance.

Andrew Griffiths

For the loves of my life, Lalita, Lala and Leo.

First published in 2020 by Andrew Griffiths

Andrew Griffiths Enterprises Trust
PO Box 6281
South Yarra VIC 3141
www.andrewgriffiths.com.au

A catalogue entry for this book is available from the National Library of Australia.

Paperback: 978-1-922391-51-3
Hardback: 978-1-922391-57-5

Printed in Australia by McPherson's Printing
Project management and text design by Publish Central
www.publishcentral.com.au
Cover design by Julia Kuris, Designerbility
Author photo by Jason Malouin, The Portrait Store

The paper this book is printed on is certified as environmentally friendly.

Disclaimer

Contents

Part VIII: Now we are convinced of the reasoning, we need some rules to work with 181

Part IX: The process we need to follow 201

Part X: Now it's time to rethink what we say 223

Part XI: More ways to increase your credibility, trustworthiness and 'buyability' 261

Introduction

Someone has to be the most expensive, why not make it you?

But if you're going to be the most expensive
you have to be the best.

What exactly made you pick this book up? What was it about the title and the overall concept that resonated with you? I'm guessing something about it might have put a smile on your face at first, but then the full impact of the title struck a little deeper. I'm guessing you've been in business for a while, perhaps a long while, and you've reached a stage where you feel like you're working really hard but not achieving what you want to achieve. Specifically, you might not be earning what you want out of your business, and it seems that no matter what you try, nothing really changes.

Feeling stuck? You're not alone

Don't worry, you are most certainly not alone. I'll explain how I came to know that in a minute, but right here, right now, I'd like you to read through this list of questions and see which ones you agree with:

- Are you really good at what you do and extremely proud of your work?

- Do you work incredibly hard, and have you done so for a long time?

- Are you are committed to constantly getting better at what you do?

- Does it feel like the financial struggle always comes back, no matter what you do?

- If your business was more successful, would you be able to do a lot of good for others?

- Is being acknowledged and treated with respect for your work important to you?

- Do you tend to discount your products or services?

- Is your reputation vitally important to you?

- Do you want to stop the constant hustle (a word I'm well and truly over)?

- Are you are starting to lose the passion for your business?

- Are you starting to wonder if things will ever change?

- Do you find yourself wondering why everyone else's business seems so much easier to run and way more profitable than yours?

Any of these ring a bell for you? If you're reading this book, I'm sure many of them sound familiar.

The reality is that many business owners feel the same. It's often thought that simply working harder is the answer – but it's not. From my experience, it's time to kick back against the backseat Uber commentators telling you to hustle more, to scale more, to get a billion followers, to spend more on SEO or whatever today's fad business strategy may be, and – of course – to make sure you are building an empire.

Remember, these people make their money out of telling you what to do and selling you their products.

There has to be a better way, right?

There are vast numbers of businesses around the world hungry for an alternative, because working harder and harder is simply not doing it for them and there is a growing sense of frustration. Imagine if there was a better option, one that got back to some fundamentally sound business practices but still took into consideration the clear reality that we are living in a very tech-based, dynamic and rapidly evolving world.

Just hustling more is not the answer.

Just scaling is not the answer.

Just posting on social media is not the answer.

In among the confusion that comes with doing business today, there is most definitely a trend starting to emerge, and this is the push back against all the 'just hustle more', all the 'scale at any cost', all the 'grow an empire'. It's about building a business that serves *you*, not the other way around. It's about building a business that is solid and that has substance. And much, much more.

This is about building a business that's as big as you want it to be, not as big as you think others want it to be. It's about a business where you get to do what you do, really well. It's where you attract customers who value you and what you do and how you do it, and they are prepared to pay accordingly. It's where new customers find you, because of your reputation, and they seek you out from every corner of the world. It's where your business gives you the things you want out of life. It's where you can give back and support others because your business allows you to do that. It's about feeling energised and excited about your business every single day. And it's about knowing you really are good at what you do and not being ashamed to say it.

All too often the image we painted of how we wanted our business to be in the early days is very different to the reality of the business we've created or that we've ended up with. My passion is to help people get back to the business that inspires them, fires them up and gives them a life of meaning and purpose.

My concept is very simple: someone has to be the most expensive, why not make it you? But if you *are* going to be the most expensive, you also have to be the best. And that's a very big 'but'. This simple but incredibly powerful shift changes everything – and many very smart entrepreneurs around the world have cottoned onto this strategy as the one that solves all their issues and finally helps them build the business they actually want.

Like many big ideas, it seems incredibly simple, and of course it's very easy for me to just rattle it off, and say now off you go – go and be expensive and the unicorns and bunny rabbits will come running to make everything perfect. In reality, it's a hard shift, especially if you have issues around money, a lack of any other kind of strategy or business model, and the (very common) self-belief that tells you people will only pay 'so much'.

Today I'm an Entrepreneurial Futurist; I get to travel the world, talking to, working with, and observing all kinds of trends in business, in particular small business, and seeing what is working and what is not. I see the emerging trends, the innovation that is happening with businesses in every corner of the planet and across every industry, and I get to draw out and analyse the common characteristics of these and put them into a format that other business owners can learn from.

Without a doubt, one of the biggest trends I'm seeing is a slowing down of business, driven by a desire to specialise, to niche, to deliver higher quality and higher value products and services and to be paid accordingly. This is a trend happening across all age groups and in all industries, and it represents an extraordinary opportunity for the committed business owner in today's rapidly and constantly evolving world. The concept of 'someone has to be the most expensive, why not make it you?' is, in my opinion, the best way to futureproof your business and protect yourself from the economic roller-coaster ride of the modern world with its recessions, pandemics, terrorism, natural disasters and so on.

So who is this Andrew Griffiths guy anyway?

But before we all start logging onto our websites and adding lots of zeros to the ends of our prices, I'd like to go back a step and share a little of my story and how this book evolved.

I bought my first business 35 years ago. I was 18. I had no idea what I was doing, as shown by the fact that I bought a SCUBA diving school and retail shop over 30km from the ocean (I like to think I was actually ahead of my time, getting in early to take advantage of rising sea levels that would ultimately make my store ocean-front). To say I had a steep learning curve is such an understatement that it's almost ludicrous to say it. Like most business owners, I leapt in and then started figuring out what the hell to do afterwards. What a fertile ground this creates for making monumental mistakes. That said, I don't think I would change any of them, but at the time they caused a lot of pain and angst, and with the wisdom of age, when I look back I see just how predictable they all were.

I've had many other businesses since that time. I've written thirteen bestselling business books sold around the world, delivered hundreds of keynote presentations to millions of people everywhere from Australia to England, India to Iran, Japan to Malaysia. I've been interviewed countless times by the mainstream media around the planet and written thousands of articles analysing what it takes to succeed in business. All of this has been my commentary on the extraordinary world of business, small business in particular, and I continue to have a fascination for the extraordinary way that creativity and innovation flourish in this space.

I've had the enormous pleasure of working with literally thousands of small business owners, helping them to build strong, solid businesses, with many growing into big corporations, and more than a few growing back into a smaller business. Over the years I've seen business evolve in extraordinary ways. The internet arrived, the fax machine died, innovation became the most searched word on the thing we lovingly know as Google. Technology has transformed how we all do what we do and social media has forever changed the way we communicate. And as consumers and buyers of products and services, we've never had so much choice and so many wonderful ways to spend our hard-earned cash.

As an Entrepreneurial Futurist I get asked to share my experiences and observations on how the world of business has changed and what I predict it will look like in the coming years – or in other words, what is the future of business? A big topic indeed. I'm asked to predict what the businesses of tomorrow will look like, and at the same time provide advice on how we can futureproof ourselves as business owners, entrepreneurs and even corporations to make sure we make it there.

One of the most profound quotes that I often use in my presentations is from Alvin Toffler, the author of *Future Shock*. He states:

> *The illiterate of the twenty-first century will not be those who cannot read and write, but those who cannot learn, unlearn, and relearn.*

I find these words to be so extraordinarily relevant to each and every one of us in business today. And the rate at which we have to learn, unlearn and relearn is constantly speeding up. Just as we figure something out, we have to let it go and learn something new.

From my observations, the businesses that get really good at this form of evolution are the ones that succeed, and they will continue to succeed. Unfortunately, there are so many others that simply fail to keep up, fail to unlearn and relearn, forging ahead blindly, even though in most instances they know what they are doing is no longer working. I've stood at the front of so many rooms full of business owners and corporates who all share that look, the one that says *I know the world is changing, but I can't change with it, I'm in denial, and slowly dying*.

Cheery stuff, isn't it? Of course, it isn't all doom and gloom; in fact, it's the exact opposite. I'm seeing such incredible opportunity in the business world; entrepreneurs are coming out of the woodwork, companies that are only a few years old are being sold for billions of dollars, and really smart ideas for solving old problems are sprouting up everywhere. It really is the golden age of the entrepreneur in so many ways, when anyone with a reasonably good idea and some basic communication skills can sell something to someone, somewhere. Entrepreneurialism is breaking out all over the world.

The business owner's curse

Now, out of all of this good news and not such goods news, fresh challenges versus old challenges, amazing opportunities and the overall entrepreneurial wonderland we find ourselves in, there is one reoccurring issue I see time and time again that causes more heartache, pain, business failure and overall grief than any other, and that is the curse of simply not charging enough for what it is that we do.

Now, I've gone from painting the picture of this amazing entre-preneurial universe and all the amazing opportunities, and drilled right back down to one particular issue. And I've done this for a specific purpose: because many of the challenges being faced by business owners today could be overcome if they simply learned how to charge a fair price for what they do. Yet so many don't. (And believe me, we will be talking about why they don't a lot throughout this book.)

Initially this might sound like a fairly simple issue to fix. Just put your prices up – right? But like so many things in life, what appears so easy on the surface is in fact extraordinarily complicated when we start prodding and poking deeper.

The real heart of the issue is that many people have a terrible business poverty mentality. This is ingrained; it comes from a lack of self-worth, misguided beliefs which more often than not are simply not true, and of course the catch-all, fear. Fear of *what*? Pretty much everything. This business poverty mentality manifests itself by people undercharging for what they do, sometimes to such an extent that they could never make a profit even if they were fully booked. Clearly a crazy and somewhat bizarre situation to be in.

Putting up our prices, refining our offering, telling more power-ful and more meaningful stories … these are all easy when compared to winning the battle of the mind. And if that mind has a business poverty mentality firmly ingrained, it's not going to be easy to shift.

Many business owners have one strategy that drives them – and this is to be the cheapest. This is their business plan, their marketing plan, their operational plan – everything. As long as they are cheaper than their competitors, they think they are winning. Of course, they are not. They are failing in so many ways I don't even know where to begin.

The better way

I work to a very simple philosophy: someone has to be the most expensive, why not make it you? Any business I've worked with that I've helped to transition from being the cheapest to being the most expensive has experienced such life-altering results, it's astonishing. But to be the most expensive, you also have to be the best. Simple as that.

Now I'm sure some of you are reading this and thinking I couldn't possibly understand how complicated your industry is, and how competitive it is, and how budget–driven your customers are. What would I know about *your* business? The idea of being the most expensive is a death sentence, right?

Well, I grew up with a poverty mentality and it certainly carried through into my early business days. I had no other strategies except price. And as a result, I had a business that made no money, no matter how hard I worked. I fried myself, working full-time hours in the business and holding down a full-time job for years, but I just kept going backwards and I was doing a good job at killing myself at the same time. I simply didn't know any other way. Keep working harder and everything will work out just fine.

Fortunately for me, I attracted some mentors who understood the concept of charging what they were worth. Their attitude to money was so vastly different to mine; whereas I never had enough no matter how hard I worked, they always seemed to have plenty and their businesses boomed. I quickly realised my issue was not so much what I was selling, but my own internal poverty mentality that was manifesting in my business, with what I sold, what I charged, my awkwardness with having money conversations, chasing debts – money, money, money.

This book has one very clear purpose: to help anyone who is sick and tired of working like a dog, never making any money and always being stressed and exhausted, to turn that around. I've done it and redone it, numerous times. I've learnt to value myself and what I do and to charge accordingly. The difference this has made in my life has been extraordinary.

I'm going to share many stories to illustrate why we need to shift from being the cheapest to being the most expensive, or as a minimum, charging what you are actually worth. And if all you get out of this book is that you simply start charging more for what you do, and you overcome all the inner talk and the stories you're telling yourself that are actually wrong, I'll be happy. And I'll be happy because I know the impact this will have on your life overall.

I'll share some of my experiences, one in particular where I tripled my hourly rate and attracted far more customers than I could ever have imagined. I'm going to talk through the major caveat behind this principle: it's OK to be the most expensive, but you have to be the best. What does this really mean? How do we define what being the best looks like?

I will also be giving you a very clear process for making the transition to charging what you are worth. It's a 10-step process, and it's certainly not one for the faint of heart. The fact is that most people with a poverty mentality in business (and in life) won't have the courage to do what I suggest. Well, maybe not at first, but when you get desperate enough, when you get sick and tired enough, when you are finally ready to make this change once and for all, because the option of doing nothing is so devastating, that's when the change begins.

Two things I'd like to add before we start down this new road. Please don't think for one second that you are alone. Of all the business issues I've encountered over the years, this is without doubt the biggest, most commonly occurring and the most difficult to shift.

Secondly, if you do make this move, and go from being the cheapest, or totally price-driven, to being the most expensive, or at least charging what you are worth, so much will change in your world. When you actually start making money at a level that you deserve, when your business attracts a better calibre of customer, when you are no longer struggling to pay your bills, when you can actually take a decent holiday without worrying about the business, when you can do the things in your business that you are good at and that you love doing, you will fall back in love with your business and your life. And that will be a good day.

Someone has to be the most expensive, why not make it you? But if you *are* going to be the most expensive, you also have to be the best.

It's time to get this rock show on the road.

Part I

THE BIG WHY ...

One thing I've discovered in life
is that the bigger the why, the smaller
the obstacles tend to be.

Where are you now on your road to becoming the most expensive?

PART I: The BIG why ...

PART II: The world has changed – have you?

PART III: There are many very good reasons to be the most expensive

PART IV: How scared does this idea make you?

PART V: So what does it actually mean to be the best?

PART VI: Does this concept really work for any kind of business in any market?

PART VII: Surely the online world is completely different? Or is it?

PART VIII: Now we are convinced of the reasoning, we need some rules to work with

PART IX: The process we need to follow

PART X: Now it's time to rethink what we say

PART XI: More ways to increase your credibility, trustworthiness and 'buyability'

Part XII: This road is not for the faint of heart

LIKE MOST THINGS in life, we are unlikely to really achieve what we want unless we've got laser-like focus on what our big *why* actually is. I think that in business we can lose track of this; we can even forget why we started our business in the first place. What I'm really trying to do in this part is to help you reflect on your business as it is today and provide an aspirational, new-and-improved option for what it could be. And hopefully this will give you the inspiration and the courage to do what needs to be done.

1

Do you have a poverty mentality in business?

We all have a money mentality;
some focus on abundance, some focus on lack.
It is a choice.

This is the most logical place to start. I'm sure you've heard the term 'poverty mentality' or 'scarcity mindset' somewhere in the past. People like T Harv Eker, Napoleon Hill, Louise Hay, Gary Vaynerchuk, Tim Ferris and many others have been talking about it and writing about it for years.

So, how do you best *describe* it? And even more importantly, what do you do about it?

It's probably easiest for me to describe how I see it manifesting in businesses all over the planet. And don't worry, I know what a poverty mentality is because not only have I worked with many thousands of people who have it, I battled it myself for many years.

The typical signs of a poverty mentality

The typical signs of a poverty mentality or a scarcity mindset in business are:

- not charging enough for the service or products being sold
- difficulty (and I mean real difficulty) having conversations about money

- a belief that our business will never be financially successful
- offering discounts for our products or services before we even get asked for a discount
- giving a discount just because someone asks for one
- a mentality that we have to work really long hours, for very little money
- finding it hard to speak up and ask for what we want in a negotiation or partnership
- a perpetual fear that everything is going to come crashing down around us
- a fear of losing our customers overnight
- nervousness and anxiety when a new competitor enters the market
- real resistance to putting prices up, even if you haven't put them up for years
- a form of depression where you think the struggle will never end
- changing direction in your business just as you're about to be successful (self-sabotage and poverty mentality often travel hand in hand)
- chopping and changing everything in your business all of the time, never giving products or services time to actually work
- the limiting belief that this is all our customers can afford to pay.

Do any of those sound like you? Most of them? *All* of them? I know it's not sexy or politically correct to think for a second that we aren't all amazingly upbeat and perky every minute of the day as we go from hustle to hustle. After all, it's all about attitude, right?

Well, to be honest, much of it is. But if you've been battling a poverty mentality in business (and if you've got it in your business, you've got it in your life overall) for a long time, you know how

exhausting it can be to feel you are never going to break out of the breakeven cycle. You're generally getting by with just enough, but no more.

Now, don't beat yourself up. As I mentioned in my introduction, it is ridiculously common, and this state of mind puts up all kinds of barriers, blocks and nasty little challenges that actually prevent us from being abundant in our business.

If you're reading this and thinking you don't have a poverty mentality, or imposter syndrome, or scarcity thinking, I can't for the life of me understand why you need this book, because if you are truly unburdened, you would already be confidently charging what you are worth, and perhaps you are the most expensive and the best at what you do.

For the rest of us mere mortals, admitting that we've got a problem is, as clichéd as it sounds, the perfect place to start our journey together. Once you accept the issue at hand, we can start to move beyond it. I know: I've been there. And I have to work not to slide back there when I'm going through a challenging time in my life or my business.

The big problem is that having a poverty mentality in business clearly leads to heartache and grief, and my biggest desire is to help as many people as possible to move beyond that place of shame, frustration, exhaustion and overwhelm. There is a much better option, believe me.

My main point here is simple and tragic: a poverty mentality tends to manifest itself the most when it comes to what you charge for what you do. And typically, this means gross undercharging, because we don't believe we deserve to be paid more. And that in turn leads to all kinds of things, most of which I'll scare you with in the coming pages.

2

But surely if you do all the right things in business that will negate the impact of a poverty mentality – right?

The greatest business strategy can be
undone by a poverty mentality.

I f only this were true. From my experience, a small percentage of
business owners are able to really forge ahead and build an abundant and profitable business while battling a poverty and scarcity
mentality. At some stage though, it always seems to rear its ugly head
and bite them on the bum.

You really need to address this issue once and for all, and I know
that's not easy. It will take time, and a fairly major commitment,
and all kinds of comfort zones will need to be shattered. And in all
likelihood, it will be something you need to work on for the rest
of your life. I know I do. But if we learn to really value who we are
and what we do, and we start to charge accordingly, and people buy
what we are selling, the road gets easier.

Is your business broken?

Another common issue I come across when I'm working with
businesses, either as a coach or as a consultant, is that their business
model is broken, limited or basically non-existent. They may be
working to a model that was fine a few years ago, but it now lacks
relevance in a modern and dynamic world. Many internal issues are

soon revealed, and most simply stem from no one actually taking the time to ask bigger, better and more relevant questions, such as:

- 'Why do we do it this way?'

- 'What is our strategy behind doing this?'

- 'What would happen if we stopped doing this?'

- 'What would happen if we started doing that?'

- 'We think this is true, but is it really?'

- 'How do we really know our customers want what we are selling?'

- 'What are we doing to make sure we are staying relevant to our customers?'

One of the interesting by-products of having a more profitable business – which generally comes from both charging more and cutting costs, and introducing simple but powerful business practices – is that *everything* starts to get better. We can afford more and better support, we can buy better equipment, we can afford to take better care of ourselves, we can invest in growing and learning instead of just spinning the hamster wheel.

What I'm trying to say is that if we change how we charge, many of the other issues within our business get fixed as a by-product. And I've seen this so often. I've worked with and watched so many business owners discover their self-worth and apply it to their business. They start to stand a little taller, they dress a little better, they invest back into their business, and everything goes up notch after notch. Every part of their business and their life improves, and that is profound.

3

The vast majority of businesses are fighting it out at the cheap end of town

The only winners at the cheap end of town are the customers, and it's a hollow victory to say the least.

Something I've observed in the work I do is an increasingly large number of businesses fighting it out at the cheap end of town, with only a handful of businesses enjoying being at the top end of the pricing spectrum. I've found this to be true in virtually every city I've visited, across all industries.

I think this is a part of the overall entrepreneurial renaissance we are in at the moment, where lots of people are starting businesses either as an option to a traditional corporate career or as a sideline with the hope of eventually making the business a full-time gig. Regardless of why someone is in a business, the current advice that new businesses are getting is, in my view, very often badly skewed.

There is so much talk about start-ups, hustling, funnels, scale and turnover – and very little discussion about actually making money or the one word that defines a business from a hobby or a charity and that is PROFIT. Being cheap seems a good way to get market share. It's such a short-term strategy that leads to disaster, time and time again. For established businesses, they may have dropped their prices over time because their market has become more saturated and they feel their only option is to reduce their prices to compete.

Whatever the reason for being there, the cheap end of town is not a good place to be, and as you read through this book, I'm going to do my best to convince you of this point. Is this true for all businesses across all industries? I'd have to say yes. It doesn't matter what the industry, if pricing is freely determined, I do believe that being the cheapest is a terrible strategy. I've consulted and coached businesses in just about every industry imaginable, and I've yet to find one that I think falls outside of my thinking around this attitude towards pricing.

To me, trying to compete on price alone simply shows a lack of imagination, especially when we are living in a world where, now more than ever, people are actually prepared to pay for quality. We have the tools and the resources to track down the specific items and services that we value (think about how and what you buy online now as opposed to a few years – or even a few months – back).

A two thousand dollar meal?

Charging what you are worth takes courage, but it also takes imagination, it takes creativity and it takes passion. Look at some of the greatest restaurants in the world. One that comes to mind for me is Masa, a Japanese restaurant in New York City. A good meal for two with drinks can cost around two thousand dollars. Now that might sound crazy, but it's always booked out, the food is apparently amazing, and the overall experience is one that has people who have just paid two thousand dollars for their meal raving about it. How good can a bit of raw fish be? Clearly it can be really good.

Now I'm not saying you need to become that extreme in what you charge, but then again, if you're good enough at what you do, and if there are plenty of people you can reach who are willing to pay for your products and services, why not?

Whenever I see any kind of business open its doors and start their marketing campaign by shouting in their advertisements that they are the cheapest, I wonder how long they will be in business. Generally, not very long. Of course, there are plenty of expensive

restaurants that close down as well, but from my experience they go broke for different reasons, predominantly not managing their costs.

The main point I want you to take from here is that the most competitive space for the majority of businesses is in the cheap end of town. This works for some: think fast-food brands. Breaking away from the pack is part of our strategy and that isn't always easy to do when you sell hamburgers.

But right here, right now, imagine how you would feel if instead of slugging it out with a pile of competitors, slashing your prices just to get a sale, working with people who show no real loyalty to you no matter how hard you try, and who don't appreciate the extreme level of service you offer and the value you bring, you consciously change your world to one that is far more rewarding.

Imagine you are working with customers who gladly pay what you charge because they value you, they appreciate you, they are loyal to you. In fact, they generate all of your work because they tell their friends, who – just like them – appreciate and value the quality products and services you sell. Imagine if every new customer walking through the door was actually your ideal customer? Not someone who wants to haggle with you on price? Or complain about the most ridiculous of things?

Now imagine that your bank account is reflecting this shift in customers. I bet it feels nice, really nice. What a far better alternative this is compared to where you may be right now.

The cheap end of town is like the roughest neighbourhood in a city; avoid it at any cost because you are bound to get into trouble.

4

You can thrive being the most expensive – but there is a big catch

From my experience, people love the idea of being the best or charging the most, but few are really prepared to do what it takes.

This is the entire premise of this book, and it's a simple premise. Someone does indeed have to be the most expensive, why not make it you? It's a simple question, and one that I think warrants a simple answer.

So many businesses under-charge for what they do, to the point where they can never really make a decent profit, so they just scrape along, barely existing – they would be far better off getting a job and working for someone else.

I work directly with people who live like this. And as soon as I ask them if they would be prepared to put up their rates, they generally come out with a whole pile of reasons why they couldn't possibly charge more – all kinds of arguments to do with the challenging times their community is facing, the increased competitiveness, the internet stealing business, and the list goes on and on.

These reasons are generally nothing more than red flags that tell me they are struggling with confidence, or they lack the energy required to make the changes they know they need to make, or they simply don't have a strategy to start charging more. Old habits become very hard to break. The stories we tell ourselves become increasingly powerful, especially when we've been telling them for years and they are often supported by other people.

I do think there is such a thing as 'small business misery syndrome' – where you get a few small business owners together and, before long, the conversation turns to how tough things are, the challenges of the times, the government, customers, suppliers, and on and on it goes. Misery does love company. The moral to this is the minute you find yourself in a small business misery huddle, get the hell out of there. No good comes from it, except reinforcement of the limiting ideas that are already causing a great deal of grief in most businesses.

So while I say someone has to be the most expensive because I love that concept, what I really want is for you to start charging *what you are worth* – even if that *doesn't* make you the most expensive – and most of us struggle with that. Yet I've never, ever, made this recommendation to someone who hasn't been able to dramatically increase their rates successfully.

So ... what's the catch?

So, what is the big catch? If you *are* going to be the most expensive, you also have to be the best. This is a line you will read often throughout this book, because the whole concept is dependent on being committed to this. People are prepared to pay for quality – now more than ever. But no business that charges the most yet delivers the least is ever going to be successful in the long term.

5

Does this story ring any bells for you?

Have you got the customers you want or the
customers you've simply ended up with?

read a story a little while back about a therapist who had reached
a challenging point in her business. She was fully booked most of
the time, and she had no real prospect to grow her business. But
that wasn't the real issue. The big problem was that she had two very
distinct types of clients.

The first always showed up early, they were polite, friendly and
professional. They took her advice, they valued her and they gladly
paid their bill at the end of every session. They would have referred
more of their friends to the therapist but she simply didn't have any
capacity for new patients.

The second type of clients was not as positive. They were always
late, often not even showing up or having the courtesy to ring.
They were rude, unprofessional and sometimes argumentative. No
matter how hard she tried to help them, they didn't really value
her advice. Then when the sessions were over, they never had the
money on them or a credit card, and she had to continually chase
them for payment.

In her ideal business, she would simply have the first type of
client happily paying a fair price for the value of the service she was
providing. So, she made a bold move: literally overnight she doubled
her hourly rate. I love that she did this, but it was a very scary thing
for her to do. And there were consequences.

A sensational outcome

The first thing to happen in the following weeks was that she lost half her clients just like that. But which clients do you think she lost? Yep, you got it, the ones she needed to lose, the terrible ones, the difficult ones, the ones who showed her no respect, who stormed out the minute they heard about these new and outrageous fees.

Now she suddenly had a practice that only had half the clients but she was still making exactly the same amount of money. Surely that's a great outcome, right? But wait, there is more.

Her great clients were also very happy with the change. They never liked it when they interacted with the not-so-great clients, often having to wait because of their tardiness or seeing the way they treated the therapist and her receptionist. Even better, her great clients could now recommend their friends and colleagues to the therapist that they loved and respected so much.

Within a couple of months, she was fully booked, with only great clients, having doubled her income and sacked the clients she should never have taken on board in the first place. Now that is a sensational outcome, and it illustrates my point exactly.

How many of us churn along, day after day, held in a business rut by our own limiting beliefs, lacking the courage to do what it takes to change our business forever in a way that works for us?

6

Put this book down now, find a quiet space and get very clear on your big *why*

The one thing small business owners don't
spend enough time doing is 'deep thinking'.
Especially about the things that matter,
the things they can actually influence.

'm pretty certain that you've heard about, read, seen or absorbed via osmosis Simon Sinek's work on starting with *why*. It seems so ridiculously obvious now, and in many ways it wasn't a new concept when Mr Sinek started telling the world about it, but no one before him had explained the concept and the process so wonderfully well. It applies perfectly right here.

If you don't have a very big why, very clearly imprinted on your brain, I guarantee you won't follow through with the process that I'm unleashing in this book. It's challenging, it's scary, it's so far out of most people's comfort zones that their toes curl just thinking about it, and that means without the right conviction, whenever the wheels start to wobble on the wagon, these people will stop and go back to underselling themselves, competing on price and undervaluing what they do.

An essential ingredient

You need a very big why to make this work. I read a quote from Tony Robbins recently that went along the lines of 'to make great changes in our life we require either desperation or inspiration'. How beautifully true is that? I look back on my life and think about the times that I made very big changes and yep, I was either over-the-moon inspired or plain terrified about what would happen if I didn't take action and create the change I needed, right then and there.

You need to decide which of those two it will be for you. It really doesn't matter, as long as the big why is *giant*. I've been the owner of a poverty-based business. One that constantly struggled to make ends meet. One that was exhausting, frustrating, all-consuming and unrelenting. And I've also had businesses that have been built on a 'charge what I'm worth' mentality, or an abundance mind. They have been joyful, rewarding, profitable, fun and invigorating. I know which option I'd prefer.

So before we go any further, I need you to stop, put this book down, and think long and hard about why you want to charge what you are worth. And you need to write this down. Put post-it notes all over the wall. Record a video for future you. Be crystal clear about why this change needs to happen and what your life will look like if you make it a reality, and what your life will look like if you just keep plodding along the way you are.

The reality is very few business owners have the courage to head down this path or to see it through to the end, and that's because it's not an easy route to follow. If it was, everyone would be the most expensive and this book would be pretty much redundant.

I'm going to talk a lot about the need to be courageous when following this strategy, so don't worry – it won't be the last time you hear about it.

THE WORLD HAS CHANGED – HAVE YOU?

'The illiterate of the twenty-first century
will not be those who cannot read and write,
but those who cannot learn, unlearn, and relearn.'
Alvin Toffler, Author of *Future Shock*

Where are you now on your road to becoming the most expensive?

PART I: The BIG why ...

PART II: The world has changed – have you?

PART III: There are many very good reasons to be the most expensive

PART IV: How scared does this idea make you?

PART V: So what does it actually mean to be the best?

PART VI: Does this concept really work for any kind of business in any market?

PART VII: Surely the online world is completely different? Or is it?

PART VIII: Now we are convinced of the reasoning, we need some rules to work with

PART IX: The process we need to follow

PART X: Now it's time to rethink what we say

PART XI: More ways to increase your credibility, trustworthiness and 'buyability'

Part XII: This road is not for the faint of heart

I'M PRETTY SURE that by now, you, like the rest of us in business, know and completely understand that we are living in a world that is spinning ever faster, to the point where doing business feels like we have the proverbial tiger by the tail every day. It's intense to say the least, and the reality is that it's only going to get more intense in the coming years.

How has it become intense? The rate of change is without a doubt a challenge. Keeping up with technology is a challenge. The change in consumer needs and expectations is a challenge. Finding enough time in the day is a challenge. But all these day-to-day struggles also have an upside – they are creating opportunity for the smart business owner who is prepared to zig while everyone else is distracted by other less important and less strategic issues. Is your business getting ahead, or even keeping up?

To me, 'change' is such a reactive word. Something happens, we have to change. It lacks strategic thinking. I'm a much bigger fan of the concept of 'considered evolution'. This is when we proactively and strategically grow and develop in a constantly shifting world in a way that makes us far better able to survive and thrive in the constantly evolving environment.

In this part I'm going to talk about some of the main changes we are starting to see in the business world and what these changes mean for us – everything from the concept of 'newism' to the hipster revolution.

I'M PRETTY SURE that by now, you, like the rest of us in business, know and completely understand that we are living in a world that is spinning ever faster, to the point where doing business feels like we have the proverbial tiger by the tail every day. It's intense to say the least, and the reality is that it's only going to get more intense in the coming years.

How has it become intense? The rate of change is without a doubt a challenge. Keeping up with technology is a challenge. The change in consumer needs and expectations is a challenge. Finding enough time in the day is a challenge. But all these day-to-day struggles also have an upside – they are creating opportunity for the smart business owner who is prepared to zig while everyone else is distracted by other less important and less strategic issues. Is your business getting ahead, or even keeping up?

To me, 'change' is such a reactive word. Something happens, we have to change. It lacks strategic thinking. I'm a much bigger fan of the concept of 'considered evolution'. This is when we proactively and strategically grow and develop in a constantly shifting world in a way that makes us far better able to survive and thrive in the constantly evolving environment.

In this part I'm going to talk about some of the main changes we are starting to see in the business world and what these changes mean for us – everything from the concept of 'newism' to the hipster revolution.

7

Customers are in the driver's seat

Those businesses that underestimate their customers have very limited futures.

There is absolutely no doubt that today the customer is well and truly in the driver's seat, and in my opinion, rightly so. We all have a world of choice when it comes to buying anything, and we are not afraid to use this choice. There was a time when competition was limited, mainly by geography. How far would we travel to find a better price or a better product? Today we are all buying things from around the planet, on a daily basis, whether it be a physical product like a book or a digital product like Netflix.

As consumers, we know how to use the internet. We are smart and sophisticated and we have so many resources at our fingertips to help us find whatever we want, wherever we want it and whenever we want it. Never before have we had this kind of commercial power.

Interestingly enough, this has highlighted what I believe to be one of the biggest marketing issues facing many businesses – they underestimate their potential customers. Accountants tell us that they do tax, lawyers tells us that they do law, mortgage brokers tell us that they get us loans – we already know this. But if you go to ten random websites for any service provider, they will basically tell us what we already know.

The same applies to products like hotels. If you go to almost any hotel website, they are basically identical. You could change the hotel name in the header and it would still work.

Today consumers are much more informed, aware and smart – and discerning, and frankly, sick of being treated like idiots. So the problem here is the hotels are sharing the wrong information. As consumers, we want to know much more about who you are in your business, why you started, stories around your people, your products, your dreams and aspirations. Leave the obvious stuff hidden deeper in your website, not page-one stuff. I feel a rant coming on … the best way to nip it in the bud is to simply say, treat your customers with the respect they deserve, as aware, informed and educated people who are becoming increasingly discerning about who they want to spend their money with.

We love everything new

Because customers have changed, we have to ask ourselves if we have kept up. I find a lot of businesses that I've worked with who have been around for a long time find this a challenge, to say the least. They want to do things the way they used to do them and, sadly, that no longer works. This is the battle for relevance – and every single business is fighting it, whether you realise it or not.

We love everything new – in fact, it is a global trend called 'newism'. This incredible thirst for all things new manifests in many ways; think about the constant barrage of new phones, new tech, new food, new products, new places, new treatments, new, new, new. We love, crave and demand new from the businesses we buy from. And this is significant for every single business owner out there.

There was a time that simply being in business for many years was all the credibility we needed to attract customers. We would proudly hang the shingle or heritage logo saying something like, 'Proudly operating for 50 years'. And to be honest, that really was enough credibility. But today, with the advent of generational marketing, not everyone looks at a business being around for a long time as enough of a credibility factor to buy from them. In fact, in many instances, it's a turn off – simply because there is an association that being around for a long time means old and stuffy and not really up to speed.

When I'm speaking about this topic at events with a mixed audience that generally consists of baby boomers and millennials (gen Y), I ask a question. If you received a terrible diagnosis of a brain tumour and you had two surgeons to choose from to get the nasty little bugger out of your head, and the first had been operating on people for 30 years and the second had just graduated from the top training facility in the country, who would you choose to operate on you and why? Baby boomers always say the experienced surgeon, millennials always say the new grad. Baby boomers love experience, millennials love the latest knowledge and expertise.

Now there are exceptions to the above, but overwhelmingly, I get that response. And this of course creates all kinds of problems and complexities when we are marketing to a number of different generations, but difficult as it may be, we need to do it. The moral to the story is simple: if you're hoping to attract more millennials than baby boomers (who, while they may be the more affluent, are slowly but surely becoming extinct), marketing your business on the fact that it's been around for a long time is not going to be enough.

This is a wonderful opportunity for brave business owners

Customers are prepared to look deeper to source the best business, product or service for their needs – and their needs are changing, along with their expectations. (I'm going to talk about these throughout this book in more detail.) The main message I want you to take from this chapter is understanding that consumers are changing, and that's providing those of us in business who are brave enough with a wonderful opportunity to actually charge what we are worth, because there are always going to be those customers who want the best and they are prepared to pay for the best, and now they can find us relatively easily.

One last note I'd like to make here is that many of you reading this book will be in the B2B space, or business to business. It's easy to think that changes to customers or consumers don't affect you because you are selling to other businesses. Be warned: that is most definitely not the case. In every business-to-business transaction there is a customer making a buying decision, and the trends that impact them in their personal life are always going to come into play in their business life. The concept of consumers being in the driver's seat is exactly the same for businesses being in the driver's seat. The same rules apply for business to business and business to consumer.

The bottom line: the customer is well and truly in the driver's seat. They hold the power and they are most certainly not afraid to use it. We can either be scared by this and run to the safe space of being the cheapest, and fight it out with everyone else in the same pig pen, or be courageous and smart, and charge what we are worth, and attract those customers who are willing to pay accordingly.

8

We think we live in a price-driven world but actually we live in a value-driven world

'The bitterness of poor quality remains long after the sweetness of low price is forgotten.'
Benjamin Franklin.

This is one of my fundamental observations from the work I do around the world – never before have we been so acutely aware of the concept of value compared to price. I often hear people talking about how price-driven their customers are, but I believe that they are actually value-driven more than anything else.

We all want value for money – and we know that the cheapest rarely gives that. In the words of Mr Benjamin Franklin, who had it pegged all those years ago, 'the bitterness of poor quality remains long after the sweetness of low price is forgotten'.

There will always be people who want the cheapest, but do you want them as your customers? That's the big question we need to be asking ourselves here.

Consumers are more informed than ever

One of the big changes in the world of buying anything is our increasing level of awareness about how we spend our money. We've all made purchases online only to receive the item and be totally disappointed with it simply because it is nothing like it is supposed to be. Or booked into a hotel that has a fantastic online presence, boasting pictures of incredible views and room facilities, only to find out that the photos used are not of your room type – you are more in the broom closet category. In other words, we are used to being ripped off and we're not happy about it.

We want, expect and demand value for money – and we are prepared to pay for it. Sure, there will always be those who want the cheapest, but there are a growing number of people more than willing to pay for quality. They are not afraid to pay more as long as they get value for money.

The types of businesses I am seeing start up now are not offering cheap products and services, they are in fact offering exactly the opposite – they are offering higher priced products and services, that are high quality, because they know that as the world becomes more affluent, which it is, there are more people willing to pay for quality.

Even when you get into the realm of the super expensive – the $100,000 walking stick, the million-dollar car, the $5000 phone – there is no shortage of customers willing to buy these products because they know they are quality.

We are becoming far better educated about the food we put into our body, the clothes we wear, the cars we drive (or the cars that drive us), the places we choose to holiday and the activities we do when we are on holidays – this global increase in knowledge is making the difference between quality and lack of quality very clear. It means that as consumers we can make better decisions about everything. And as far as I'm concerned, we want value for the money we spend more than anything else – and therein lies the opportunity: the more value you provide the more you can charge.

9

Thank goodness for the hipster revolution

*Find a business being run by hipsters and
just sit back, look, listen and learn. Leave your ego
at the door, they've got more than enough for all of us,
but appreciate what they bring to the table without
really knowing it. Here is your key to the future.*

In the past 10 years we've well and truly seen the rise of the hipster entrepreneur. Personally, I love them. They bring some flair and attitude to the small business scene, and in many ways they've made it cool to be a business owner once again.

Hipsters started in the food scene, naturally enough, but now I'm working with hipsters running accounting practices, vet clinics, schools, gyms, marketing companies, gardening businesses, removalist businesses, law firms and pretty much every other industry. And they are revitalising the way we do business around the world, and because of that I think that we have a lot to thank the hipsters for.

How hipsters have changed business forever

They have changed a lot about the way we do business and the way we think about business. I love the energy they bring to doing business and the fun they have brought back to the small business space. I think there are 10 specific reasons why we should be grateful to small business hipsters everywhere and welcome the hipster revolution with open arms:

1. *It's now very cool to do one thing and do it really well.* If you want to do nothing but sell great coffee or make a particular type of food or collect honey – and nothing else – that is now absolutely OK. In fact, we love businesses that do one thing really well. Hipsters get this, and they are very happy to find that one thing and do it better than anyone else.

2. *We don't all have to be building an empire.* For a while there it seemed that if you were in business and you didn't want to sell it for a billion dollars in a year, you simply weren't trying hard enough. Now hipsters have helped us come to terms with the fact that not everyone wants to build an empire, but if you do, that's OK too. The bottom line: build the business you really want, not the kind of business that others expect.

3. *People love personality and hipsters have plenty of personality.* I think business was getting a little bland for a while. Everything was starting to look the same, like one big franchise. Hipsters have come along, covered in tattoos, beards and funky clothes, embracing their individuality and encouraging it in their staff. They have personality and they aren't afraid to use it. It just goes to show that customers want to do business with people who have personality. I know I do.

4. *It's nice to do things that take time to get right.* In a world obsessed with fast, a lot of hipster businesses are fighting back and taking the slow approach. They do things well. They don't advertise that they are the fastest, instead they actually say they do it right, not fast, so if you want fast, go to a bland, faceless business.

5. *People will pay for quality.* Hipsters have a laidback approach to doing what they do, but don't for a second think that translates into a 'we don't care' attitude. From my experience hipsters are incredibly committed to quality. They know that modern consumers are prepared to pay for it – and at the same time

they know that as the world becomes more competitive, a lack of quality will be punished mercilessly.

6. *It's nice to smile when you walk into a business.* Every time I walk into a hipster-run business I can't help but smile. They are having fun, they can have a conversation with you, they are proud of what they do and how they do it, they have a wonderful sense of team and they laugh a lot. Who doesn't want to buy from a business like this?

7. *Hipsters have taught us to be fearless.* With everything from food trucks to mail order razor blades, hipsters are all about giving it a go. If it doesn't work, you pick yourself up, dust yourself off and try the next idea. They don't spend years beating themselves up. They try new things, they love new ideas – the more innovative and offbeat the better. They teach us to not be afraid of giving a business idea a go – but do it well, charge what you are worth and let your personality shine through.

8. *Hipsters know how to tell stories.* With storytelling again at the forefront of marketing, hipsters know how to tell meaningful stories that count and that get attention. They tell the personal stories, the real stories, and the stories that their customers engage with.

9. *They know the importance of doing good.* Hipsters don't need to be told that they should do good, help others, support local charities, make a difference, do the right thing, protect the environment – and so on. They naturally do all of this because it's a part of their DNA.

10. *Hipsters are not afraid to charge what they are worth.* I went into a barbershop in Melbourne recently, a hipster haven, and they charged $75 for a shave. Now there was a time when I would have laughed, saying there is no way anyone would ever pay that kind of money for a simple shave. But of course, it is far from a simple shave – and there is a line out the door, with people waiting up to an hour for a shave. People will pay for quality – hipsters are proving that in every industry.

So next time you see a hipster business, find a quiet spot and sit and observe. We can all learn a lot about doing business in the modern world from our hipster brothers and sisters. I love them and what they have brought back to the world of small business in particular. Don't be afraid of letting some tattoos, piercings and vintage clothing into your business.

10

If your entire business strategy is to be the cheapest, you're in for a hard road

Being the cheapest is simply a lazy strategy,
that rarely, if ever, pays off in any shape or form.

A s I've mentioned a couple of times, I completely understand why many business owners adopt a strategy of being the cheapest. Sometimes it's all we know (it certainly was for me when I started in business). Often it's out of fear as more competitors enter the market, it feels like something we can influence quickly and effectively in a simple message ('we are the cheapest' rings out as a pretty good sales line when we are not sure what else to say), or we simply don't have a better alternative strategy to grow our business.

Herein lies the big issue – the reality of having a strategy based on being the cheapest generally leads to a fundamentally flawed business model, to the point where the business's long-term (and short-term) viability is questionable.

My personal – terrible – experience of being the cheapest

From my personal experience of running businesses when I thought it was all about being the cheapest, a number of things were constant:

1. I never actually made any profit because I simply didn't charge enough. I broke even, for years, but there was never any left over and it didn't seem to matter how much I sold.

2. I never had any money in reserve, because of the point above. So I had no fat to get me through any lean times, or to deal with any setbacks, like broken equipment, tax, Christmas and so on. To survive I had to borrow more money, or as many businesses do today, live off an ever-increasing mountain of credit card debt.

3. I always struggled to grow because I was constantly undercapitalised. The only way to grow was, you guessed it, get deeper in debt.

4. I always felt like I was fighting a battle just to stay afloat. And it was a battle, all day, every day, year after year. This is a terrible way to live.

5. Most of my business decisions were fear-based – not a good place to make decisions from.

6. I attracted totally price-driven customers, and that leads to all kinds of issues (which I'll cover in more detail in the next chapter).

7. I had challenging relationships with my suppliers because I was constantly in a cash flow crunch which made it really hard for me to pay my bills on time. This was both embarrassing and stressful.

8. I had no real point of difference when it came to marketing my business – except to say, 'I'm the cheapest', which was pretty much what everyone else in my space was saying.

9. I couldn't afford good advice. In fact, I couldn't afford *anything*. So I just kept doing what I always did and getting what I always got.

10. I felt like I was stuck. It didn't seem to make any difference how hard I worked or how much I sold, I never had any money left over at the end of the week, and the slightest hiccup – like a bad debt or extra expense – threw my world into chaos.

I don't mean to nag, but seriously, this whole 'be the cheapest' is quite simply the worst business strategy you can have. It's important to me that you know I understand what it feels like to be stuck in this loop, and clearly I have been there. But my big drive is to help you break out of it. And I'd like to say it's easy, but it isn't.

Being the cheapest *is* easy, but to what end?

11

What happens when you attract customers based purely on price?

Cheap customers refer their cheap friends.
The more cheap customers you have the
more you will have. Like always attracts like.
Time to attract better customers.

've spoken about what a 'being the cheapest' business looks like, I've lived it, and I see many businesses that still run on this principle, and many more that maybe don't have the 'we are the cheapest' slogan but they are very much price-driven in their outlook, to the point where they never charge what they are worth. I've also made mention of the point that when we have a cheap mentality we attract customers with a cheap mentality, but what does this really look like?

When I finally started to charge what I was worth, the single biggest thing I noticed was the calibre of the clients I attracted and how that changed dramatically. This was in a marketing business I had started. Initially I had priced myself at the lower end of the market, and most of my customers were small business owners who could barely afford to pay – and who often *didn't* pay.

When I changed my business model entirely and literally became the most expensive (and I'll talk about this transformation later in the book), I started to attract bigger clients, with healthier marketing budgets, with a much more realistic attitude towards what they would pay for my services. And of course, they then recommended me to more of their associates, and the transformation was complete.

It was a beautiful thing to watch. I moved from totally price-driven, cheap clients, where I continually struggled to make ends meet, to more professional, affluent clients, with a high sense of commercial respect and a willingness to pay well for quality advice and service. And both of these types of clients were still small businesses – just very different ends of the spectrum.

I absolutely love it when I help other businesses have this transformational experience.

The negative effects cheap customers have on your business

But back to what it looks like when we build a customer base purely on price, and in this instance, customers wanting cheap, cheap, cheap. Typically this is what having a cheap customer base looks like:

1. Cheap customers have no lower limit; no matter how cheap something is, it's not cheap enough. So you'll often find yourself acting like you are running a business in Bali where everything is a negotiation, regardless of the fact that you've clearly stated your prices.

2. Cheap customers don't value your products, your services or you.

3. Cheap customers rarely have any true sense of loyalty other than supporting you because you're cheap – in other words, if someone else comes along who is cheaper, you're out.

4. Cheap customers tell their cheap friends about your business – so you keep getting more and more cheap customers. Awesome.

5. Cheap customers are the most likely to complain – about everything. They want a Maserati product for a Hyundai price.

You get the drift I'm sure. There will always be a market for people who want the cheapest, but is that the space you want to play in? In part III, I'm going to talk about the real benefits of charging what you are worth and, ideally, becoming the most expensive in your industry. And that's the cool and exciting part of this whole concept.

Put an end to the struggle, stop underselling and undervaluing yourself, and find the right customers who will appreciate you and what you do. Once you do this, everything changes.

12

There is a wonderful freedom when you accept that not everyone is your customer

One of my greatest business breakthroughs
was having enough self-respect to say no.

One of the fundamental aspects of starting to charge what you are worth, as opposed to charging what you think people will pay, is that you soon realise not everyone is your customer. And in fact, your ideal customers probably represent a small fragment of the total customers available to you.

This shift means we stop focusing on trying to get 'everyone' and really target our marketing on getting the *right* customers. Not a new concept I know, but to be honest, how often are we targeting our marketing around those who will value us, be prepared to pay accordingly, have the capacity to find us and maturity to work with us to solve whatever problems they may have? Or do we go back to the sticky point of price?

When you embrace the concept that not everyone is your ideal customer, and you are OK with turning people away simply because they are not right for your business, the evolution to charging what you are worth starts to happen. Some people in business get this concept right from the beginning, and most of us start our business with high ideals but quickly adopt an 'anyone who has a pulse is now my customer' approach – and that's when things start to go awry.

One of the most rewarding aspects of this transition to charging what we are worth is that we naturally start to select both the customers we really want and should have and those that we need to part company with. Don't worry, more on that later in the book. But for now, imagine how your business would look if you just had person after person as your ideal customer? Sounds too good to be true, right? It's not.

Who is your target market *really*?

As a small business author I often have people say to me, 'Obviously your target market is small business owners'. My response is, 'No! My target market are motivated, energetic, smart business owners who are absolutely passionate and driven to build truly successful businesses on many levels.' Clearly that narrows down who my readers actually are – and who my clients actually are.

For many years I would work with any small business owner who simply couldn't pay – and I ended up with the business I deserved as opposed to the business I wanted. I'm pretty sure you can imagine what that was like – I was earning lots of good karma and becoming the Mother Teresa of the small business advisory world, but I was going broke rapidly.

Know who you really want as customers, get crystal clear about that, and never be afraid to say to a prospective customer, 'I just don't think we are the right fit for each other'. You can always throw in a 'it's not you, it's me', if that will soften the blow. I've done it many times.

This really is one of the fundamental keys to this concept overall. If your business philosophy has been all about having a price-driven strategy (aka being the cheapest or undercharging for your products and services), then I'm pretty certain the customers you have today will mostly be gone when you adopt a new and improved strategy.

My whole point is that we need to be confident enough to charge what we are worth, we have to be good enough to deliver on our promise, we have to exceed expectations in every way – and then we have to find the right customers, and as I've mentioned many times, they probably aren't the ones you have right now.

There really is a perfect storm happening now – we are able to communicate globally, social media is a fantastic tool, there is a growing affluence in the world, consumers are embracing 'new' and understanding the concept of quality more than ever – and they have the tools, the resources and the motivation to find those businesses that tick all the boxes for them. Geography is becoming less important by the day.

We need to be really clear about the kind of customers we want, versus the kind of customers we have, because if we aren't careful we will end up with the customers we deserve.

13

Expense without quality just doesn't work

I'm not going to pay $25 for a Big Mac.
They know it, you know it. Expense without quality
is a surefire recipe for disaster.

et's summarise and make sure we are on the same page (so to speak). I've done my utmost to explain that fighting it out at the cheap end of town is not a good business plan. In fact, it's a horrible strategy overall, yet so many businesses end up there. My whole mantra in this book is that someone has to be the most expensive, why not make it you – BUT, and it's a giant BUT, if you *are* going to be the most expensive, you also have to be the BEST. Now, I talk a lot about what being the best actually means a little later in this book, but I want to introduce the concept here.

If you want to build a business where you can charge what you are truly worth, and customers are lining up to do business with you, you have to deliver. It's as simple as that. And as complex as that.

And while delivering is the goal, is it really enough? In my view it's not.

Satisfaction is not good enough

The key to having satisfied customers is to meet their expectations. Do this and you can charge accordingly. But the key to being the most expensive and doing it successfully is to *exceed* their expectations. Blow them away. Have them raving about what you do to anyone who will listen. Do that and you will win on both counts – you'll be able to charge what you want *and* you'll have a procession of customers lining up.

Down the road from me is a small bakery. It's called Tivoli Bakery, and it's little more than a hole in the wall with a few seats, down a side street in suburban Melbourne (food capital of the planet, I might add). Yet from 7.30am every morning, like zombies, people start appearing from apartments, houses, alleys and Ubers, arms outstretched, all ambling to Tivoli for their fix of incredible bread, baked goods and coffee.

Twice a year Tivoli Bakery makes two special products – in the build-up to Easter they make hot cross buns, and in the weeks before Christmas they make mince tarts. Both of these products are ridiculously good – and ridiculously expensive. The hot cross buns are around $5 *each* (you can buy a pack of six hot cross buns from a grocery store for around $3.99, so $30 for six versus $4). And the same with the mince tarts: a six-pack from Tivoli is $25 – a six-pack from a grocery store is around $6.

Now, don't get me wrong, I'm sure the grocery stores sell plenty of packs of the cheaper product, because there are always going to be people who want the cheapest, but Tivoli Bakery sells thousands and thousands of super-expensive hot cross buns and mince tarts every year, because they are exceptional quality and they exceed customers' expectations (the first time they try them). And Tivoli sells out of these products every day in the season. People pre-order them by the box load. Who wouldn't want to be able to sell a premium product to a long line of customers willing, and in fact over-the-moon happy, to pay for them?

The moral to my story is very simple. You can't charge the most for an inferior product or service. And whether it's inferior or not value for money is judged entirely on whether or not your customers' expectations are exceeded.

And this is where this entire premise can get bastardised. A business tries to charge more for what they do; in fact, they make themselves the most expensive, but they simply can't deliver.

We've all experienced this in a restaurant or a hotel. In this instance, charging what you are worth should be the approach. If you can't make a decent product or offer a great service of some kind, charge appropriately. That's a big reason why the likes of McDonald's offer cheap food – because no one is going to pay $20 for a McDonald's burger, simply because it isn't worth it. Expense without quality is a recipe for disaster. Simple as that.

Part III

THERE ARE MANY VERY GOOD REASONS TO BE THE MOST EXPENSIVE

Create an aspirational future so incredibly compelling that you have no option but to be drawn towards it.

Where are you now on your road to becoming the most expensive?

I'D LIKE TO TAKE a few pages to dive a little deeper into the upside of charging what you're worth and ideally becoming the most expensive in your space. I need to spend time really working through all angles of this strategy. We need to deal with the benefits as well as the demons that stop us from charging what we are worth.

14

If what you're doing isn't working, this is the opportunity to take action

So many businesses are working with a broken model.
Yet no big, hairy or audacious action is being taken
to fix what's broken.

I'm sure you've heard the saying, 'if you keep doing what you've always done you'll keep getting what you've always got'. And this rings incredibly true in business. If you've been doing what you do for some time and you're not really getting ahead financially, and you're feeling the pinch, getting exhausted and a little fed up, you have the option to keep doing what you've always done, but what's the real likelihood of that working?

If there are good signs of growth and your business is heading in the right direction, then yes, absolutely, now it's more of a time game, getting to where you are going as soon as possible. There is light at the end of the tunnel. But if you're not really moving any closer, and you're being honest with yourself, it might come back to two simple choices: shut up shop or try something more radical.

The diving store nowhere near the ocean

I'd like to share a story with you about my first business. As I mentioned in the introduction, when I was 18 I bought a dive shop. It was located 30km from the ocean (I wonder if there is any issue with that?), and built on a total poverty mentality.

I ran my dive shop exactly how you would expect an 18-year-old kid to run it, which is to say exactly the same as the man he bought the business from. I bought this business from a crazy Canadian called Mac, who lived from hand to mouth and much preferred smoking joints and sipping Canadian Club Whiskey on a daily basis rather than actually working, selling dive equipment or teaching people how to dive.

I had no idea about profit and loss, mark up, cash flow, or any other fairly basic business acumen. In fact, I became good friends with my bank manager because every day he would pop in and give me the cheques that I had bounced the day before.

The real problem was simple: no matter how much gear I sold, my prices were way too cheap and there was really no way I would ever make a profit. It took someone else to help me realise this.

One of my suppliers often came to my shop for a coffee and a chat on his way home. He would look at my shop, my customers, my empty cash register and shake his head. He kept telling me that I sold the worst equipment, simply because it was cheap. And it was both cheap and nasty, often getting returned due to faulty production and materials. But selling cheap gear was all I knew.

My dive courses were cheap too. The reason they were cheap was because I priced them the same as every other dive shop in Australia (and ironically, most still charge the same amount today, 35 years later – what does that tell you about this industry?).

And in the midst of all of this, I kept losing money, slowly going broke, week after agonising week, month after agonising month. Ironically I had plenty of people coming into the store and buying various bits of equipment, but as you know by now, just because I was selling stuff didn't mean I was making any money.

Then something strange and wonderful (or so I thought) happened. I won five thousand dollars in the lotto – and rather than use that money wisely, I decided to spend it and get some business advice from a complete stranger. So I made contact with a man who had been recommended to me. He assured me he could save my business from impending disaster, and his fee (surprise surprise) would be five thousand dollars, which I handed over blindly, thinking that my windfall must have been some kind of divine intervention.

He spent a few days hanging around the shop, talking to my dive instructors, my customers, my suppliers and of course my bank manager. Then he gave me a list of instructions. At the top of the page were the following words: 'Andrew, someone has to be the most expensive, why not make it you? But if you *are* going to be the most expensive, you also have to be the best.' Sound familiar?

I didn't realise how powerful those words would prove to be.

He gave me a list of changes I needed to implement – and my spirits sank:

1. Halve the amount of stock you carry and double the prices.

2. Only carry premium equipment that you would use.

3. Stop selling dive gear on credit.

4. Get rid of the fish net and plastic crabs on the wall
    (all dive shops need these decorations to survive; it was
    just common sense).

5. Turn your dive shop into a dive boutique.

6. Double the price of your diving courses.

7. Get your dive instructors to wear suits and become
    'dive consultants'.

8. Change the name of your business.

9. Offer incredible service, and I mean incredible.

10. Commit to being the absolute best dive school and retail
    store in Australia.

As I read through the list, I realised I had just wasted my last five thousand dollars. What this consultant was recommending was simply ludicrous. There was no way it could possibly work; after all, a dive shop with no fish nets or plastic crabs on the wall? Absurd. I was devastated.

I didn't make any of these changes. I knew they would never work. My dive shop looked like every other dive shop, sold the same gear as every other dive shop, charged the same as every other dive shop. I just needed more customers and that would solve all my problems.

So, in my infinite wisdom, I continued going broke.

A few months later, I actually hit my real rock bottom. I was completely skint, in debt way beyond my eyeballs, and I could see no way out. In a final act of desperation, I pulled out the list my consultant had given me and thought, 'What the heck, I'll go down swinging'.

Having no money made this extra challenging, but somehow I begged, borrowed or stole paint and new carpet, some stunning marine life pictures and a beautiful three-metre-long fish tank built into a sales counter. We painted the walls and laid new carpet ('we' as in whoever I could recruit to come and give me some slave labour). We disposed of the fish nets and the plastic crabs. I got rid of the cheap and nasty stock, and somehow struck up a deal with a new supplier of quality equipment and fitted out my dive school with state-of-the-art gear, all on credit.

Then I doubled the price of everything including my dive course, held my breath and reopened the business.

The grand reopening

From day one the results were simply amazing. We had become a diving boutique. We were expensive, but we were the best. We had long conversations about what being the best meant and we stepped up fully. We lost a lot of our old customers, who only came to my store because I was cheap, but we attracted a pile of affluent new customers who loved nothing more than buying expensive dive equipment and taking expensive dive holidays.

In one weekend we sold 200 wetsuits, which was simply crazy. Before the transformation I would have been lucky to have sold one dodgy wetsuit a month.

My business was transformed, and I was amazed. But what was even more amazing was that the new customers I attracted were looking for quality and they were prepared to pay for it. They understood *value* as opposed to *price*. They could easily have bought what I was selling more cheaply, but they saw value in what I was offering beyond just the product. I believe we became the best dive shop in Australia.

A few weeks after reopening, my consultant came by. He could tell things had changed simply by the number of people in the shop and the smile on my face. He reminded me of his statement: 'Someone has to be the most expensive, why not make it you? But if you *are* going to be the most expensive, you also have to be the best.' And I've done my utmost to live to that code for the rest of my life.

Now your job is to make sure you are always the best.

15

Twelve very compelling reasons
to be the most expensive

This has nothing to do with greed,
it has everything to do with self-respect.

I like the idea of lists. A simple, nice, easy-to-get list that spells out all I need to know. I thought it would be compelling if I could give you a simple list to showcase the 12 benefits of charging what you are worth and, ideally, being the most expensive.

Here we go:

1. You will attract a whole new range of customers who are prepared to pay you what you deserve to be paid.

2. These customers will tell like-minded friends and colleagues about your business — which will result in you attracting more quality clients like them.

3. You will be appreciated and valued for the products and services you sell.

4. New, often unimagined opportunities will begin to flow your way.

5. Your word-of-mouth recommendations will increase because your reputation will grow.

6. These will be cleaner recommendations, meaning people already know you are good at what you do, so you don't need to sell yourself.

7. Your business will become more profitable (or at least profitable at long last).

8. You will have more money to do the things you really want to do.

9. You will have more money in reserve for those times that you need it.

10. You won't need to work as hard as you probably have been in the past.

11. Your health and wellbeing will change – because your state of mind will be so much better.

12. You will get that excited feeling about your business back.

Another reason, which I haven't put on the list but I just love, is that when you are the most expensive, you actually get to throw a lot of the business rules out the window. If you build a rock-solid reputation for being the best at what you do, and people are tracking you down, you can play a little more exclusively. Let me share an example.

Being the best in the business

I've worn glasses for many years. When I was in my early twenties I realised I needed glasses because I literally had to pull over on the side of the road, get out and walk up to street signs to try to navigate my way around. I cringe thinking about the menace I must have been on the road. Anyway, I finally got glasses and I've worn them ever since.

For those of us who wear glasses, they soon become an extension of who we are – they are part of our personal brand. Buying a new pair of glasses is a big deal that is both exciting and a chore. About 10 years ago I was presenting at an event in San Francisco, having a little downtime, wandering around the downtown area. I was walking by a small optometrist store and a very cool pair of glasses caught my eye.

I went inside and started talking to the salesman. He was flattering, telling me what a good eye I had for quality glasses. Anyway, he gently took the ones I liked out of the window and brought them over. I tried them on, and fell instantly in love. They were very cool, big, black, with chrome on them, just a little rockstar (which is so *not* me), but super cool in every way. The brand was Chrome Hearts – and I'd never heard of them before. Then he told me the price and I nearly passed out.

They were thousands of dollars. Without lenses. I had never in my wildest dreams considered paying that much for a pair of glasses, but the more I looked at them, felt their quality, saw the craftsmanship and just noticed how incredible they felt on (yes, glasses can feel incredible on), I knew I had to have them. This started my love affair with Chrome Hearts.

I travelled back to Australia, nursing my new acquisition, still shocked at how much I had just paid for a set of black glasses with a bit of bling on them, got new lenses (which cost a thousand dollars because these frames are difficult to fit – of course). And I finally got to wear them. And strange things started to happen.

Firstly, they quickly became a part of my brand, to the point where I have a logo of my face and glasses. The number of people who complimented me on my glasses was amazing, and still is. And complete strangers would come up to me in airports, at events, or even reaching out through videos posted online and ask me if my glasses were Chrome Hearts. There was a kind of secret club of people who, like me, have become aficionados.

As you do when you start to fixate on something, you research. I soon discovered that Chrome Hearts break just about every business rule: it's impossible to buy their glasses online (they simply don't allow it); their website is so weird and eclectic, you wouldn't even know they sell glasses; and it takes months to get a repair. After 10 years of wonderful use, my original Chrome Hearts needed some work. I sent them away six months ago and will possibly get them back in the next three months (and they unashamedly let you know this).

Everything about this brand is attitude. They are undoubtably one of the most expensive eyewear brands on the planet. They are only stocked by a handful of retailers in any particular country. They are incredibly well-made from the absolute best materials. And the people who buy them will buy them till the day they die, regardless of the price.

A few months back I bought a new pair; they were nose-bleed expensive and I absolutely love them. I would never consider buying another brand.

Chrome Hearts break so many business rules – but are they successful? Hell yes. Are they futureproofed as a business? In my opinion, absolutely. Who wouldn't want a business like this?

So the point here is simple. I'm sure you've got it loud and clear by now: there are many, many, many good reasons to be the most expensive. All you have to do is be the best.

16

Are you making a lot of assumptions about your customers and what you think they will pay?

The 'charge what you think they can pay' strategy is as bad as the 'be the cheapest' strategy.

As you'd expect, I often have conversations with business owners about what they charge, and many of the same arguments about what their customers can or cannot afford to pay come up. And I talk about this and other customer-related assumptions in various guises throughout this book. But the one I want to talk about specifically here is the underestimation of our existing customers, let alone all the new ones who are out there waiting to buy from us.

Many business owners base their pricing either on what their competitors charge or what they think their customers are prepared to pay. Both pricing options are pretty flawed, in my opinion. If your prices are being determined by your competitors – who could have totally different cost structures, operating expenses, financing, other sources of income and so on – you're basing your pricing on their world. What if you're wrong? And believe me, I have worked with businesses who if they were fully booked would still be losing money because they have never really worked out their costs in a more realistic and strategic way.

Think about that for a second, as I'm not exaggerating in the slightest. I've worked with business owners who even if they were at one hundred percent capacity, their businesses would lose money. How on earth is that possible? They simply haven't done their numbers correctly. They have pulled prices out of thin air, based on nothing more than what their opposition charge. And they have years of not making a cent to look forward to, until finally they shut the doors.

And trying to decide how much your customers are willing to pay is likewise a guess and a terrible way to do your pricing, yet so many businesses do it. And once again, I see more businesses getting this wrong than getting it right. There is no solid foundation for charging this way, and most of the businesses that do this dramatically undercharge, which of course leads to all the dramas that we've spoken about already.

My advice here is to make sure that when it comes to pricing, you do it strategically. Be smart about it. Yes, charge more – please do, by all means be the most expensive – but base your pricing on some sound business reasoning.

This means you need to know your numbers really well, and sadly this is still a challenge for many business owners. Do you know exactly how much it costs you to operate every single day, week and month? Do you know your hourly operating cost? Do you know if you're making money or losing money right now – as in, did you make money *today*? And if you did, how much did you make, exactly? Waiting to work this out at the end of the financial year is lunacy. Yet I often encounter business owners who sometime in July announce to the world how much money they made last financial year. Bugger that; to me a smart business knows how much money it made or lost every day. I don't need an accountant or even a piece of software to tell me that. That's the level of knowledge we all should have when it comes to having a very firm grip on our business finances.

Taking responsibility for your business

This is often about stepping up and taking responsibility for your business. I learned the hard way that I had to do this. I once got into big trouble with the Australian Taxation Office and a terrible business partner, which forced me to put my business into the hands of an external administrator. I had to have a hearing with the ATO – which is like getting a colonoscopy without anaesthesia.

I remember telling the lovely folks from the ATO all of my woes, all of my challenges, how difficult everything was, the horror of it all. At the end of my Academy Award–winning presentation, they said, incredibly matter-of-fact, 'Andrew, that's a terrible story, but we don't care. When are you going to pay your tax bill?' And just like that, I realised I had to step up and take responsibility for my business, and that starts with taking financial responsibility. Those lovely ATO peeps did me a big favour that day and I've never looked back.

So I took control of my business from a financial point of view. I knew that I was responsible for every bill, for every invoice, for every cent that I owed in tax or other responsibilities – and I had to change. In the past I had been mostly in denial about things like that. I'd leave it to the bookkeeper or the accountant to manage those things, but at the end of the day, they had no responsibility for any financial aspect of my business – I did. So I took control.

I started to get to know my numbers. I learnt to read a profit and loss sheet and a balance sheet (no matter how ugly either of those may have been). I got to know exactly how long each of my customers took to pay their accounts, and how long, on average, it took me to pay each of my suppliers. And what this actually meant. As I mentioned earlier, I learned exactly how much it cost me to run my business for an hour, a day, a week, a month and a year. I knew how much money I needed to have on hand to keep the doors open. I knew how much I owed, and how much I was owed. I knew how much I had to put aside for tax and things like holiday pay and superannuation. I dissected every product and service I sold – and quickly worked out why I never had any money. My most popular services were the least profitable. Once again, you get the drift. And while I digress a little, moving to a 'charge what you are worth' model will work much better when you know your numbers.

Another really interesting observation of mine came when I was working with my former wife in our marketing company. Carolyn has a big history in advertising agencies in capital cities. She worked on big product launches for organisations like BMW and many other luxury brands in various capacities. She has a very well developed sense of commercial value.

Now in our office, I tended to do the quotes. And a lot of my early thinking was around 'what can the customer afford?' Carolyn's was not. She knew the value of our work, she was not afraid to charge, and she had no doubt that we were the best at what we did. So I had quoting responsibilities taken away from me. And I was rarely shown any of the quotes that Carolyn did.

Time and time again, until it was the norm, she quoted three, four, five times what I would even consider quoting, and we always got the quality jobs. We had a reputation – we were the most expensive, but we were the best. It's not an easy sentence to say, but it says a lot. You need a high degree of confidence to pull it off, but once you do, everything changes. Carolyn taught me a very valuable lesson in the 'charge what you are worth' school of life, and I'm extremely grateful to her for that.

But back to my original point of this chapter: question the assumptions you make about whether or not your customers can afford to pay more. From my experience they will, across every industry, as long as you give great value and exceed expectations. Don't underestimate your customers and their loyalty to you, even as you change your business model. Yes, you will lose some, maybe a lot of your existing customers, but the point I come back to is that you will tend to lose the customers you need to lose.

Think back to my earlier story about the therapist. She lost half of her patients, but they were the half she needed to lose. The ones she kept were the good ones, who valued her, respected her and gladly paid the higher fee, and who could now refer other high-quality patients like themselves.

17

What happens when you become the most expensive with a reputation to justify it?

Seen on a New York City subway in the
midst of the Global Financial Crisis:
'self-worth is more important than net worth'.

A lot starts to change internally and externally when we successfully make this leap. You'll get the feeling for the internal shift as we move through the book, but one of the nice shifts is what happens externally – with something called 'opportunity flow'.

When I've been stuck in struggle street, undercharging and living the full-blown business poverty life, it felt as though getting every cent was a battle. In fact, it felt like *everything* was a battle, full stop. But when I've built my reputation, profile and credibility, instead of constantly chasing work, it comes to me.

Now, I'm not saying you don't have to market yourself, or be active on social media or work hard; what I'm saying is that you start to get recommended a lot more by others who acknowledge you for being really good at what you do. The opportunity flow changes from a constant hustle to the ongoing management of opportunities coming your way.

This only works of course if you've got the reputation to back up the prices you charge. Not a lot of people come rushing forward to work with someone who charges the earth and fails to deliver. (We are going to talk about the concept of 'being the best' later.)

Simply the best

A line I've heard many times, typically in a new client meeting, is: 'I've heard you're expensive, but you're the best. I only want to work with the best.' I'm very happy with that. I'm not concerned in the slightest that someone says I'm expensive. That part is nowhere near as important to me as the 'you're the best' part. That means I've built up my reputation and I have to deliver, which I'm confident of always doing.

For some of you reading this book, the thought of someone saying you're expensive might send a shiver down your spine, but don't worry, you will learn to love hearing that. People will track you down to work with you. And now, thanks to the wonderful world of the internet, it's not hard to find anyone.

That is such a fundamental shift – the ability for anyone to track us down, find out more about us and buy from us, whether that be a product or service. Now we can all pretty much do business with people anywhere, so in many instances, that means our potential client base. By that I mean those people who really are prepared to pay us what we are worth – is so much bigger and so much more accessible.

And of course, there are the new opportunities that are drawn to people who are really good at what they do. The potential partnership opportunities, the media opportunities, the bigger client opportunities – the list goes on and on. The key here is the hand-in-hand link between what we charge and our ability to deliver. If you can do the latter, you're guaranteed of being able to do the former.

18

How would your life really look
if you took this step?

Sometimes we become so comfortable with
the present that no matter how bad things are now,
we stop imagining what the future could be.

What I would love you to do now is to close this book and put it down. Grab a pen and a notebook (writing stuff down is much better for your brain than typing it on a device), find a quiet place or go to that special place that you love, and spend as much time as you need to think long and hard about how your life would look if you made the change to your business that I'm suggesting.

Finding your compelling future

Perhaps asking yourself some of the following questions might help you to create a really compelling future, one that gets you excited and motivated about the outlook for your business and your life:

- What would it mean for you to stop struggling financially?

- How would you be spending time in your business if you weren't constantly doing the hustle just to make ends meet?

- How would your health be if you weren't so stressed out about money?

- How would your relationships change if your business was more financially successful?

- What would you be able to do more of?

- What would you be able to do less of?

- What kinds of clients would you attract?

- When was the last time you felt excited about your business?

- How long have you been struggling? When is enough enough?

- What kind of difference could you make to others if you had more money, more time and more energy?

- What's one giant goal that you can never imagine yourself achieving because you are always struggling to make ends meet?

You can create a far more compelling future, one that gets you excited and energised, and one that you know is possible, simply by changing how you charge for what you do. I say 'simply', but of course there's more to it than that, but what a wonderful place to start. I hope you are excited about what could be, and you're getting ready to leave that old mindset behind.

HOW SCARED DOES THIS IDEA MAKE YOU?

Fear has been one of my greatest motivators and constant companions in my business. Fear of failing, fear of succeeding, fear of not being enough, fear of losing everything, fear of being far more than I ever thought I could be. I owe fear a great deal.

Where are you now on your road to becoming the most expensive?

PART I: The BIG why ...

PART II: The world has changed – have you?

PART III: There are many very good reasons to be the most expensive

PART IV: How scared does this idea make you?

PART V: So what does it actually mean to be the best?

PART VI: Does this concept really work for any kind of business in any market?

PART VII: Surely the online world is completely different? Or is it?

PART VIII: Now we are convinced of the reasoning, we need some rules to work with

PART IX: The process we need to follow

PART X: Now it's time to rethink what we say

PART XI: More ways to increase your credibility, trustworthiness and 'buyability'

Part XII: This road is not for the faint of heart

I'M SURE YOU'VE READ the first few parts of this book with mixed feelings. You know you want to charge what you are worth, and the concept of being the most expensive is appealing for all the benefits it brings. Logically you see that: the concept sounds fantastic, you know there is a process to follow that I'm going to take you through, but that dreaded fear monster might be raising its ugly head right about now.

Fear is what keeps most of us in this poverty space and, ironically, it's a fear of poverty that makes it worse. The hardest thing you can do is make the changes I'm going to share, but deep down I'm sure you know that you have to.

It's OK if the concept of charging what you are worth sounds great, you really love it, but it scares you. And if the concept of being the most expensive takes your fear to a whole new level, even better. It *should* scare you, because this means you will treat this very seriously. And believe me, the fact that I'm suggesting – in fact, imploring – you do this is not something I'm doing lightly.

I would never suggest making the changes I'm going to recommend to anyone who lacked the commitment to make them. You can't half do this. You have to be serious and you have to be prepared to do the hard yards. This is a theme I keep reiterating throughout this book, simply because I find that there are plenty of people who love the idea of making dramatic changes in their business but very few who are prepared to actually do what it takes.

This is compounded by the world we live in – we are surrounded by weekend experts offering to transform our business and our life in about 15 minutes. It just doesn't happen this way. Having been in business for over 35 years, worked directly with thousands of business owners, and through my speaking and writing connected with millions of business owners, I know that business success is as much about courage as it is about having a great product or service. In fact, it's more about courage, hard work and persistence than anything else.

So if you're feeling scared, that's OK. I'm taking you through this process in a systematic way, starting with sharing the reality of what business looks like when we don't change enough, the benefits of changing our thinking around what customers want, the importance of value, and then we will get into the 'how to' part of the process.

19

We all want to charge more but most people don't have the confidence

One of the most courageous things you can do in business is to charge what you are truly worth.

At some stage, this is what it will get to – you know you want to charge more, certainly to charge what you are worth, but do you have the confidence to *actually do it*? It's the falter point, and it's where people tend to come up with the biggest reasons not to proceed.

The single biggest push-back I receive to this concept is, 'but our customers won't pay more'. Or sometimes it's, 'our business is in a price-driven market'. Or the other fairly common line is, 'our industry is super competitive… we have to compete on price'. I understand each of these points, I've heard them before a thousand times, and I guarantee that there is always someone who completely and successfully bucks the trend – and the rhetoric.

Let me share a story about a very good friend of mine, Peter Lik. Peter is a landscape photographer. He has been for many years. With the advent of digital cameras, everyone has become an expert photographer. It is ridiculously competitive in every way. Add to this the advent of stock libraries to buy images, and even stock libraries where you can get fantastic images for *free*, and it's easy to say that for a landscape photographer like Peter Lik, 'people won't pay much for images', 'he's in a price-driven market', 'his industry is so competitive', and so on and so on.

There's no way he could charge a premium for his photos, right?

In 2014, Peter Lik sold three images for US$10,000,000 (about A$15,000,000). One of these images sold for US$6,500,000, making it the most expensive photograph in history. Peter is without a doubt a man who lives by the adage that 'someone has to be the most expensive, why shouldn't it be you?'

Today he has galleries all over the world, million-dollar image sales are relatively common, and he has developed unique ways to sell limited edition prints to his select clientele.

Why has Peter Lik been so successful financially when there are so many photographers out there? Having seen him work, there are a number of reasons for his success:

- his incredible work ethic (without a doubt he is the hardest-working person I have ever met in my life)

- his deep understanding of his customers

- his confidence (he's a great photographer and he knows it)

- he values everything that it has taken for him to get to where he is

- he is not afraid to ask for what he feels is a fair price for his work.

Now, I get that we aren't all going to sell million-dollar images. And in many ways, Peter is somewhat of an anomaly, but year after year I've watched him build his business into a global empire by following this concept of charging what you are worth regardless of all the reasons why we shouldn't.

The stories we tell ourselves

Now, back to those reasons why we can't charge what we are worth: 'my customers won't pay any more', 'the market is too tight', 'it's too competitive', 'we have to compete on price', and so on. From my experience, these are stories we tell ourselves that generally mean we have to find new customers. And that's a big part of my strategy when it comes to charging what we are worth.

In all likelihood, if you go down this path you will need to change your customer base. And that's a little scary. When I'd had enough of selling my services for way too little in my marketing business, I literally moved to an expensive new office with no clients. That was terrifying, but also incredibly liberating. It took me an afternoon to get a pile of clients simply by knocking on doors in the building that I relocated to (and I mean literally knocking on doors – three hours of door knocking got me three years of work).

If I asked you if you are good at what you do, how would you answer? If you don't believe you are good at what you do, if that lack of confidence shines through, you will never be able to make this change. There are two options you face if that's the case:

- get good at what you do if in fact you are not good at it

- if you kind of, maybe, just a little, think you *are* actually good at what you do, it's time to change your thinking to build your confidence.

Once again, don't worry … I'm going to talk through how we make this transition. I'm just making sure we move forward from here with you being fully aware of what's involved. Being confident enough to make this shift is a battle for all of us.

One thing I have really noticed over the years is that it's much easier for me to see the value in a person and what they do than it is for them to see it in themselves. One of my greatest joys in life is to show someone just how extraordinary they are, even when I know they don't believe it. But I wear them down, I show them their value, I teach them to show others, and an extraordinary transformation begins.

20

Understanding your own poverty mentality stories and the impact they are having on your business

Our script for life is written in pencil, not carved in stone.

We all have a relationship with money of some sort, mostly formed in our early years. It's amazing how powerful this can be and the impact it can have on our lives. It only stands to reason that if you have poverty mentality stories you tell yourself, they will impact on your business.

Recently I was asked to be a guest mentor for a project in a little town called Port Lincoln in South Australia. We had about 200 kids from various schools come along for a day, to talk about money, entrepreneurialism, their community and much more. It was such a fantastic day, filled with fun activities, limitless thinking and beautiful creativity, all seen through the eyes of kids between about 10 and 15.

One of the mentors did a session on money. She put up a slide with a picture of a pile of cash and she asked the kids what that image meant to them. The responses around the room were very surprising. Words like 'fighting', 'guilt', 'selfishness' and 'arguing' came flying in from all directions. It soon became very clear that the kids' views on money were very much shaped and impacted by their parents' relationship with money and the conversations that were had at home, which were clearly not good.

You must first clarify how you see money to change your mentality

A big part of changing our poverty mentality is clarifying exactly what it is. For example, for a long time I had the belief that I always had enough money. And that's exactly what I had. I never had more, I always just had enough to get by – and I just got by. Having just enough in business is a surefire way to always be struggling.

Over the years I worked to change that. I did this by changing my definition of what 'enough' meant to me. When I was a teenager, $50 was enough. As I've got older, enough meant substantially more, and that definition change really has worked well for me. I worked not only on the actual amount that I needed for it to be 'enough', I worked on what 'enough' meant. I started to include the 'what if' scenarios, the need for thinking about the future, the desire for a better lifestyle where I got to travel more.

There are all kinds of poverty mentality stories we can tell ourselves. Again, most originate somewhere in childhood: 'money is bad', 'rich people aren't very nice', 'money is the root of all evil' (seriously, what a terrible limiting belief that one is), 'if it's not a struggle then it won't happen', 'business is supposed to be really hard', 'I'm not worthy of success', and so on.

You know what *your* poverty stories are. And if you're really honest, you know why you don't charge enough. Is it really about all the external excuses most of us throw around, or is it much more about the internal programming we picked up along the way?

Awareness is the beginning. What words do you associate with money? What are your positive experiences and what are your negative experiences? And most importantly of all, what impact are your thoughts about money having on your business – both good and bad?

21

I charged $35,000 for two days' work – and changed my entire poverty mentality

Learn to hang onto those moments where you felt truly, deeply and honestly valued by others for your unique set of skills and experience.

Becoming a professional speaker really helped me to get a better feeling of value and self-worth. I still remember the first paid speaking job I did. I remember asking for $250 for a one-hour presentation – and the client said *yes*. I almost didn't believe it. I was absolutely chuffed. Ironically this was more significant to my business than the hundreds of highly paid speaking jobs I've done since.

For most speakers, this is the biggest and most important shift they can make: to move from the space of speaking for free to being paid. It's a seemingly giant hurdle, and one that is much harder than moving from, say, $250 for a one-hour presentation to $3000 for a one-hour presentation.

About 10 years ago I was offered a speaking job that ran for two days and required me to make a number of presentations to different groups. It was a lot of work and very intense, and at the time I was charging about $5500 for a one-hour speaking gig. As this job entailed me doing about six presentations, I plucked a number out of thin air and quoted $35,000. The client agreed immediately and asked me to issue an invoice. I was stunned (as in 'jaw dropping, re-read that email over and over again' stunned).

To me this was a huge amount of money; I'd never been paid anything like that, and in fact one of the few jobs I'd ever had came with a salary of $30,000 for the *year*. So my benchmark was two days' work for $35,000 versus one year's work for $30,000. That was a good day. I went on, did the job, the client was very happy, and I've done a lot of work with them since.

There is no doubt this particular project had a major impact on my own poverty mentality. As you will see throughout this book, I've had periods in my earlier days when I battled poverty mentality, overcame it, and then slipped back into it – but something happened with this job that changed something inside me for good. I think it was the fact that my client was so ecstatic with the work I did, the value I brought to the table, and the feedback they got from their customers. In their eyes, I was worth this big fee, and I think I now believed it myself.

After this, my thought process was simple – if one client will pay that amount of money, why wouldn't another? And of course, they did.

As a professional speaker, it's easy to look at a fee of, say, $10,000 for a one-hour presentation and think how ridiculous – no one is worth that. (People like Richard Branson charge about $250,000, and Al Gore is famous for charging $1M to deliver his 'Inconvenient Truth' keynote.) But for little old Andrew Griffiths as a speaker, what is the audience actually getting? They are getting the sum of my many years of experience as a successful entrepreneur, the knowledge shared in 13 bestselling books, the observations and realisations I get travelling the planet working for all kinds of organisations from the United Nations to CBS, which I distil and present in 60 minutes. *Plus* the information I gather from working with thousands of small business owners every year, via face-to-face contact, webinars, podcasts, workshops and other events. Surely that makes a $10,000 investment a good one? It all comes back to being confident enough to ask and capable enough to deliver.

And to take this a little further, what if there are 500 people in the audience? The cost is actually now about $20 a head. Seems kind of cheap, really. Might be time to put my prices up now that I'm thinking about it.

'Why can't I have more clients like this?'

Anyway, before I descend into a self-indulgent think-out-loud session, my point is very simple. I have had many transactions over the years where people have paid me for my services. In fact, that's happened my whole life. But a few of these transactions were very pivotal to me, to the point where they shook my world and changed my poverty thinking once and for all.

You've had these moments as well. Think about those projects you had where you got paid really well, where the client really valued you and what you did, and where everything went perfectly. At the end of it all you asked yourself the question, 'Why can't I have more clients like this?' And that's exactly what we are trying to do.

Think deeply about the jobs, projects or clients that really made you ask this question. Who were they? How did these evolve? Why did you get the work? How did you pitch yourself? Did you think you would get the work? How exactly did it make you feel? What problems did it solve for you at the time? What opportunity did this work create? Is there any reason on earth why you couldn't do that again? And again? And again?

What I'm asking you to do is to stop focusing on the experiences that are holding you in a poverty mentality and focus on the experiences that can help break you free, drag you forward and change your mindset once and for all. We all have both, the good and the bad; what you choose to focus on will determine where you go from here. Make a list of the poverty mentality moments where your thinking was challenged, where you felt full of energy, hope, inspiration and joy. Create the space for more of these moments and they will happen. I know because they have for me.

22

Have you become comfortable with the struggle in your business?

'Change happens when the pain of staying the same
is greater than the pain of change.'
Anthony Robbins.

Most of us know what it's like to be in a relationship that has run its course. We know it's over but we have developed a certain level of comfort with the situation that keeps us there. The same applies to being in a job we hate; it's easier to whinge and moan than find a new job. And believe it or not, I see a lot of people in a business that is struggling, that has always struggled, often because of flawed and limiting beliefs that hold the business on struggle street, because they have become comfortable with whinging and moaning rather than doing something about it.

So the big question I want to ask here is: have you become comfortable with the struggle in your business?

Now, some of you might read that and think it's a crazy question to ask. I get that. But from my experience, there are actually a great number of business owners who would really like to be financially successful but they have actually settled into a very comfortable, never-ending struggle, where it's much easier to keep telling the story about how hard things are in business and how tough its been and the sacrifice that they have made than do something fairly significant and courageous about it. This is hand-on-heart stuff, and

I'm not judging for a second. I get it. It's hard, and I know the power of being comfortably in a negative cycle.

I used to call this the small business owner's badge of honour. You would sit in a circle with a few other business owners seeing who has gone the longest without a holiday to prove who has suffered the most. Thank goodness this thinking is changing.

Change rarely sticks unless we have a long, hard talk to ourselves

We will usually only take major action for two reasons: the first is that we finally have enough of a situation, or secondly, something significant happens that makes us decide to change once and for all. I think it's fair to say we are familiar with both. But change rarely sticks unless we have a long, hard talk to ourselves.

I often think about a friend of mine, a lifelong smoker. He got a terrible cough, and when he visited his doctor, he received the prognosis that he probably had emphysema. He walked out of the doctor's clinic, threw his cigarettes in the bin, and went off to have a series of tests. It was three weeks before he went back to see the doctor, and in that time he didn't have a cigarette and he didn't even crave one. Expecting the worst, he sat nervously in the waiting room, until finally he was called in, only to be told that he didn't have emphysema, just a bad chest infection.

Now, the doctor went on to tell him that he was on the path to getting emphysema and worse, but my friend didn't hear that. He left the clinic and bought a package a cigarettes and immediately started smoking again.

When my friend thought he was in imminent danger, he reacted immediately and stopped smoking. When he realised the situation wasn't as bad as it could have been, that the danger was probably far in the future, he saw no reason to change and went back to his old behaviours.

Has something significant happened that is going to make you change, or have you just had enough of your current situation? Either way, it's up to you to make change happen. And as per the

Tony Robbins quote 'Change happens when the pain of staying the same is greater than the pain of change'.

If you're sick and tired of struggling, or always battling to make ends meet, or feeling undervalued and unappreciated, you have to get uncomfortable enough to change. And that is harder than it sounds, especially if you've been struggling for decades. Get grumpy, get angry, get frustrated, just don't feel nothing, especially if that's what you've been feeling for years. The problem is we are often more comfortable struggling than we are with abundance. And I'll leave this chapter with that for you to think about.

SO WHAT DOES IT ACTUALLY MEAN TO BE THE BEST?

Deep down we all want to be the best,
but are you really prepared to do what it will take
to become the best and to stay the best?

Where are you now on your road to becoming the most expensive?

PART I: The BIG why ...

PART II: The world has changed – have you?

PART III: There are many very good reasons to be the most expensive

PART IV: How scared does this idea make you?

PART V: So what does it actually mean to be the best?

PART VI: Does this concept really work for any kind of business in any market?

PART VII: Surely the online world is completely different? Or is it?

PART VIII: Now we are convinced of the reasoning, we need some rules to work with

PART IX: The process we need to follow

PART X: Now it's time to rethink what we say

PART XI: More ways to increase your credibility, trustworthiness and 'buyability'

Part XII: This road is not for the faint of heart

CLEARLY THIS IS the crux of my overall concept – someone has to be the most expensive, why not make it you? But if you're going to be the most expensive you have to be the best. That's the simple truth, but of course we have to define what being the best actually means.

Regardless of whether you simply want to charge more for what you sell, or you really are aspiring to be the very best at what you do and charge accordingly, your customers are going to have higher expectations when your prices go up, and if you don't deliver the concept falls over.

We've all come across businesses that charge a lot but everything about what they do is terrible. Their service sucks, their attitude matches their service, their products might look good but fail to deliver – you would be disappointed if what they were selling was cheap, but when they are charging more than others and failing so dismally to deliver, you get angry. And that is a very significant shift.

We might go to a fast-food outlet, order a meal from the drive through, see the amazing images lining the wall suggesting fantastic-quality food, and then of course we open the bag and realise what we paid for is *nothing* like the offer. *But*, we all know what to expect and we live with the lie of the offer because we know the truth. Our expectations are low, and they are always met in these kinds of restaurants. So, we're happy to pay for our burgers and fries.

But, and this is a big but, would you pay $30 for a Big Mac? I doubt it. Would you pay $15 for a large fries from McDonald's? Absolutely not. And McDonald's knows that. They would love to charge these prices but they just couldn't deliver on the expectations of $30 burgers and $15 fries.

The world's most expensive burger costs US$5000. Yep, about $7500 Australian pesos. Where do you buy it? Las Vegas, of course. The Fleurburger 5000 can be found at the Fleur restaurant, located inside the Mandalay Bay Resort and Casino. Is it the best burger in the world? Probably. Depending on your definition of 'best'. And that is key.

Do lots of people buy the Fleurburger? You bet. It's full of the best beef wagyu steak, truffles and foie gras, and it comes with a bottle of 1995 Chateau Petrus from Bordeaux. It's not just a burger, it's an *experience*. It has incredible novelty, social media bragging, the epitome of excess oozing out of it – served in one of the most lavish restaurants in the world. Each aspect of this burger contributes to make it the best, and by association, the most expensive.

Whether or not it actually tastes the best is clearly subjective and, in many ways, completely irrelevant.

In this part I'm going to talk about what it really means to be the best. These are my thoughts; there are others of course, but what's most important is how your customers define the best. And what that means for you and your business. And that's what you need to work out.

23

There is always that one business that's considered the 'go-to' best business – be that one

Find your own charge-what-you're-worth business model.

I spent a few years working in the tourism industry, making the transition from being a commercial diver and dive instructor to being a part of the sales and marketing team for a giant Japanese company. This was in Cairns, right on the Great Barrier Reef, which is of course the best place on the planet to be diving.

When I transitioned into sales and marketing, I had to learn a lot about selling. There were three main operators running big boats out to the reef on a daily basis. Most of these big boats had the capacity to carry somewhere between 300 and 400 people. There was one company, called Quicksilver, who were easily the leaders. They were the most expensive, and they were the best. By association, they were the most successful.

Part of my sales training was to go out on our competitors' boats to see what they did better than us and what we did better than them. It soon became clear we were definitely coming in at third place in terms of the quality of our operation, the reefs we visited, our level of service, everything down to the lunch we served. Our operation lacked on every level – and seeing how good the competitors were really opened my eyes.

No matter how hard our company's management team tried, we never even got close to being at the standard of Quicksilver. Everything they did was just a cut above the rest of us, and it showed. The word on the street was simple; if you want to go out to the reef on the best operator, go with Quicksilver. They are more expensive than the rest but they are the best (the line I love, and the line that has filled their boats for years).

When referrers are saying 'you are the most expensive but you are the best', you are winning. Of course, there are plenty of cheaper options, or even mid-price options, smaller boats, overnight trips – all kinds of choices. But Quicksilver differentiated itself by consistently being better than the other big-boat day-trip companies in every way, and they charged accordingly. And they do till this day.

I spent many years living in Cairns. And no matter what you were looking for, there was always a 'go-to' business that most people recommended. There was the go-to law firm, the go-to accounting firm, the go-to graphic designer, the go-to restaurant, the go-to mechanic – and depending on who was making the recommendation, they were normally the most expensive.

Wear it with pride

Your goal is to become that 'go-to' business – and to become absolutely OK with people saying that you are the most expensive, but you are, without a doubt, the best. At first you may not be comfortable with this tag, but it won't take long to wear it with pride. When I started having people describe my marketing company in this way, I was a little uncomfortable. I heard it over and over again: 'Such and such recommended you … they said you are expensive but you are without a doubt the best.'

It scared me.

But what happened? I attracted clients who wanted the best and who were prepared to pay accordingly. That sounds horrible, right?

24

'Being the best' covers a lot of ground

*Being the best is an easy concept
but a complex reality.*

As I sat down to write this chapter, I was looking to really define what 'being the best' actually means. I started to go down the 'Webster's Dictionary defines "best" as … ' path, but I fell asleep at my keyboard. I'm not going to do that. Instead, I decided to look at what I see in the businesses I've worked with and studied around the world that are clearly considered the absolute best at what they do, and who charge accordingly.

At the top of their game

These are the characteristics, and perhaps a self-review checklist, for any business that is at the absolute top of its game.

1. They have a deep and ingrained culture that is all about being excellent at what they do

Without a doubt, these businesses have an internal culture that is absolutely, and probably obsessively, about being the best. Generally this refers to their product or service, but it tends to flow through to every part of their business. The culture is so strong that being anything but the best is not really considered an option, and it shows.

2. They are totally committed – to everything

Being 'committed' covers so much territory. The businesses that are the best at what they do have a high level of commitment to their people, their customers, their suppliers and their industry. They are loyal, they are considered. Their commitment is simply to do what they do better than anyone else – and they understand they can't do that on their own.

3. They are very competitive (like, *super* competitive)

They are competitive. Being considered the absolute best at what they do, whether it's in their town, their city, their state, their country or the world – they want to keep that title and they will work incredibly hard to do exactly that. They invest in learning, skill development, getting better and better all the time, working to hone that competitive advantage. Think of an elite athlete. These are elite businesses.

4. They are incredibly brave

Businesses that are the best have to be brave because it generally means doing what others won't do, and that feels like a lonely and isolated place for most people. To be the best means you have to buck against the norm, you have to get out of every comfort zone imaginable, and you have to be prepared to move into unchartered waters, with many obstacles.

5. They are creative

Creativity is such an unexplained characteristic and influencer in successful businesses. Living in such a rapidly changing world, one that is anything but consistent, requires creativity not only to succeed but to just keep up. They are creative with their products and services, but also with how they manage their people and their customers. They can think outside of the norm and they aren't afraid to try new – in fact, they thrive on it.

6. Their products are truly extraordinary and easily the best

Clearly the end result – the thing people buy and use – has to be the best. Whether it be a meal in a restaurant or a piece of art for the wall, or a new computer or a hotel on a tropical island or a hamburger – the product really is leaps and bounds ahead of their competitors.

7. The services they offer are at the highest professional level

Many businesses are selling a service rather than a product – does all of this 'being the best' apply here? Absofrickinglutely. In fact, I think service-based businesses have even more opportunity to charge more for what they do, because there are generally so many more opportunities to create extraordinary interactions and experiences.

8. They treat everyone with respect

While the businesses that are the best often battle with an internal love/hate relationship with perfectionism, I've noticed there is a lot of respect. They respect themselves and what they do, and by association they respect their customers and suppliers just as much. Respect is a word that comes up often in my discussions. For example, I love talking to chefs who have established relationships with suppliers who grow amazing food. There is so much mutual respect and admiration.

9. They don't just serve people, they create experiences everywhere

Businesses that are the best at what they do understand the need to create experiences, a concept that comes up time and time again throughout this book. If your business simply does *transactions* instead of creating *experiences*, you will struggle to ever become the best at what you do. But I'll talk more about this deep, deep idea a little later.

10. They are constantly evolving

Evolution – the backbone of survival. In today's business world we are all fighting a battle to stay relevant with our customers, and one of the most important elements of being successful at this is to constantly evolve. What needs to evolve? Everything. Not just the products and services we are selling, but how we do business, how we sell ourselves, our growth, our business – everything, everything, everything.

11. They deliver

This one is pretty simple – they deliver on their promises. What they say is what they do, and they have built a reputation on exactly that. If you buy a brand new Rolls-Royce, I'm pretty certain you are going to get exactly what you wanted, and every single expectation you have will be not only met but exceeded.

12. They are curious

OK, I'm going to do a little name-dropping here, but I'll do it for a point. A few years back I had the pleasure of being part of a speaker line-up at a big event that included the likes of Richard Branson and Tim Ferriss, with some 10,000 people attending. Waiting in the green room to get ready to do our various things, I had the opportunity to have a short chat to Richard Branson – and what I found humbling was while I got all giddy and tongue-tied, he started asking me all kinds of questions about my books, my speaking, doing business in Australia, flying (did I like Virgin, and what could they do better here?) – question after question. He's a curious man.

I was in Japan once on a speaking job and it was early in the morning. I had a few hours to kill and I just love wandering around the food markets in the basements of the department stores on the Ginza in Tokyo. I love that there are $200 rockmelons, square watermelons for ease of transport, fish of every kind imaginable, and mangoes being sold at nosebleed prices, to mention just a tiny bit of what is available.

As I strolled around I saw a man I recognised but had never met. His name is Tetsuya Wakuda, a very famous Japanese man who lives in Australia. Tetsuya runs extraordinary restaurants, among a host of other food-related venues from beef to beer around the world. He is very, very good at what he does.

I strolled over, introduced myself, and explained that I was a big fan of his. In true Japanese style he was very humble and courteous. I asked him why he was in the food market so early in the morning, and he explained that he loved food so much, coming to Japan always gave him an opportunity to see what was new, what people were buying, what the quality of the produce was like, and much more. It was his perfect way to spend a few hours – learning, thinking, being curious.

We were the only two people in this market, as it had just opened, and Tetsuya invited me to walk with him. He explained everything about the types of food, how they were used, where they were grown, the Japanese farming and fishing principles – and much more. His passion, his curiosity, his kindness will stick with me forever.

People who are the best at what they do have a thirsty and curious mind, which I love. It's certainly an attribute that I've nurtured within myself. When I'm being interviewed for television, a magazine or a podcast, I often get asked why I've been so successful as an author, speaker and entrepreneur. My answer is simple: 'Because I'm incredibly curious – and I'm curious about everything.'

25

It's not about being the biggest – in fact, in many instances the smaller the better

Build the business you want, not the business
you think others expect you to build.

I really want to emphasise this point – there is a perception that to be the best you need to be the biggest, but in fact I'm finding the exact opposite to be true. As consumers, we are looking more and more for the smaller, more boutique products and services, because there is often an inferred quality that goes with being smaller and specialising.

I love watching food shows, specifically travel shows featuring food – think Anthony Bourdain and Andrew Zimmern. They travel to exotic places, showcasing incredible chefs, people growing and harvesting all kinds of food, old traditions and new trends. To me, one common theme is the smaller, quality producer that gets showcased.

I remember one show that featured the Brittany region in France, an area with an incredible abundance of amazing food produced and grown by a collection of very opinionated, perfectionist-orientated and extremely passionate people.

One man was shown who made all kinds of foods, but the item he was particularly well known for was 'standing sardines'. He puts locally caught and very fresh sardines into a jar, standing upright, with a garlic clove and a few other herbs. He then fills the jar with the very best olive oil available, puts the lid on and lets them sit for six months.

When they are ready to eat, people line up to get a jar. He only makes one thousand jars per year, and when asked why he doesn't make more, especially when there is no shortage of sardines, garlic or olive oil, and no shortage of demand, his response is that if he started to mass produce, the quality would drop and they would lose what makes them special, which in his view is the ingredients combined with his process, passion and commitment. I love this approach and attitude so much. And it's becoming increasingly common.

Limited supply, absolute best quality

Limited editions. Limited numbers. Limited amount of availability. Limited seasons. I'm seeing consultants and advisors limiting the numbers of clients they work with. It's a theme I'm seeing increasingly often – with everything from food to motor vehicles.

I think this is a winning formula – limited supply, absolute best quality – and people will be lining up to buy what you are selling.

Now interestingly, we live in an entrepreneurial world where everyone seems kind of obsessed with scaling – building an empire. Personally, all I see are the remains of failed empires littering the entrepreneurial landscape, and occasionally a unicorn manages to survive.

What really upsets me is that many of these new businesses started, and they were amazing. Incredible products, cool service, innovative thinking – smart, smart, smart. Then someone gets in their ear, tells them to scale, scale, scale – and the decay starts.

The first thing to go is service; the little things that made them memorable start to slide. Then the quality of the product or service gets a little less awesome, and continually gets worse. Little by little, all the things that made the business so great at the beginning are lost, and the decay continues until the empire falls.

Never, ever be afraid of being small. All indicators are that small, niched businesses, that are exceptional at what they do, can pretty much charge what they like. Their customers will find them and keep coming back, as long as they meet expectations and, ideally, exceed them over and over again.

And if we go back for a second to my concept of futureproofing yourself, being a small, tightly run, profitable business with low overheads and plenty of money in the bank, your chances of surviving things like COVID-19 or a global financial crisis are so dramatically increased that it's almost ridiculous.

26

Being the best means being totally committed to mastery

'I fear not the man who has practised 10,000 kicks once. But I fear the man who has practised one kick 10,000 times.'
Bruce Lee.

love this concept. Being the best means being totally committed to mastery, so I guess the question is, what does mastery mean to you? Hang on, I'll get that Webster's Dictionary out again … OK, I promise never to do that. To me, mastery of anything is best described as:

Having an intense focus and ongoing study, in a particular field, over a long period of time, where momentum grows as your knowledge and experience grows, to the point where the closer you think you are getting to mastery, the more you realise how little you actually know.

Now, while I don't call myself a master, I have worked to master my skills as a speaker, author and entrepreneur for 35 years. Most days, I wake up, start to study, research and learn, and I'm reminded of how little I know – to the point I often wonder if I know less today than when I started down this path of aspiring to mastery.

That said, I'll never stop. I think it was Bruce Lee who said that the only time someone can be called a master is the day they close the lid on the coffin.

It's about never-ending learning and improvement

My question to you is pretty simple and straightforward: are you really committed to mastering your craft? It doesn't matter what your chosen craft is. Mastery is a state of mind. Part of it is about never-ending learning. Another aspect is constant and never-ending improvement. It's about being brave enough to shatter the comfort zones, to do what others are not prepared to do. And it's not something that is achieved when working 9 to 5, five days a week.

My personal belief is that now, more than ever, there are plenty of people on the planet who are prepared to pay for the products and services of those who are totally committed to mastery. And the reward, for this huge commitment, is exactly that: a business that attracts quality customers, who are loyal, who promote you, who respect you and all that you do.

Now please remember, not everyone is going to become an artist who creates works like the Sistine Chapel. Not everyone will become a Tiger Woods. Not everyone will form a band and go on to become the Rolling Stones. There are levels to mastery; what's important is the state of mind that this represents. The desire to become better.

So you may say you are committed to being the best, so you can charge accordingly for what you do, but are you really? Until you are, the rewards of being the best will remain frustratingly elusive.

27

How do you treat your customers now? And how do you need to treat your customers if you go down this path?

The day a spreadsheet is more important than a customer is the day your business is officially in trouble.

Nothing makes me quite as grumpy as a business that treats its customers like sheep, without any form of respect or appreciation. They are just another faceless customer with a wallet or a purse to sell something to. Sadly, this attitude is increasingly common, especially with online businesses where there is no face-to-face contact. But even bricks-and-mortar businesses struggle to really get the value of a culture that is all about customer respect.

Another thing I have noticed is that as a business grows, the business owner tends to have less face-to-face interaction with the customers. They spend more time out back, in a little room, looking at spreadsheets, leaving the customer loving to someone else. Big mistake in my opinion. When a spreadsheet is more important than a face-to-face interaction with a customer, your days are numbered.

When we move into the space of being the best at what we do, one thing I've really noticed is a universal attitude and culture of respect for customers.

Many years ago I used to hear about a local butcher called Gavin Marsh. He had built a legendary reputation for selling the best meat available, and I'd often hear that wonderful line, 'his meat is expensive, but it's the best'. So one day I decided to check his business out and discover if it was just his product, or was there more to this story that I could uncover?

I arrived at the business on a Saturday morning, and it was packed. The counter was literally three people deep, and it's not a big shop. There were a few butchers serving, being cheeky and doing all of the things that make a good butcher stand out. But there was one man, who was skinny, getting on in years but sprightly like a teen-ager, running around talking to everyone, grabbing meat, packing it up and doing a thousand other things all at once. But he did one thing that really made him stand out and this made me immediately recognise this man as Gavin Marsh, the owner.

As people squeezed into the shop, he immediately yelled out a g'day, mostly using the customer's first name. He held about a dozen conversations with various people, and he asked so many questions about them, their jobs, their families, their businesses, it was hard to keep up. I had no idea how he could remember so many people, let alone so much information about them. And his questions weren't generic, they were very specific. I could have watched him all day.

Now, as a newbie, he obviously didn't know me. As I hustled my way to the front, he started asking me questions: what was my name (and he reached over the counter and shook my hand), he asked me what I did, where I lived, how long I had lived in the area, what my blood type was (OK, he didn't ask that, but he asked a lot of questions), and while it didn't feel in any way invasive, I realised he was collecting data.

I bought some meat, nearly passed out at the price, went home, cooked it up and realised that yes, it was worth every cent and I'd never buy from any other butcher again. Even after I moved away from that part of Cairns, I'd drive for 30 minutes just to buy from Gavin.

But that said, the gold happened when I went there the second time. It was a little more quiet, I dropped in on my way home one afternoon to get something for dinner. When I walked in the door he picked up our conversation from where it had ended about a week before. He remembered my name, what I did for a living, where I worked, my partner's name and so on. This was truly impressive. And he didn't just recite this stuff like a parrot, he was genuinely interested in me, and it showed.

How did he do it? It felt like a scene from a movie where he must surely have a high-tech mission control centre with a team of data analysts feeding him info through a cleverly hidden ear-piece. Of course he didn't, but I had to find out why he was so good at this.

On another day, I was the only one in the shop and Gavin was also the first one there, setting things up. It was 6.30 am, which says something about his business. Who opens at 6.30 am, right? So I asked him how he did it. How had he become so good at what he does?

Gavin started to tell me about his suppliers, his great team of butchers, the fact that he owned his own farm and grew his own animals, and I had to stop him. I said I understood the quality of his meat and his people, but how does he manage to remember so much about his customers and to make everyone feel so special?

Gavin stopped what he was doing, put down whatever he was wrapping and came around the counter to stand next to me. He told me the story of the business (it was founded in 1926), and Gavin is the fourth generation to run the business. His father went to great lengths to impart a culture that was all about respect for their customers. This meant treating them like family, being there for them in good times and hard times, supporting the community, being a part of the community and so much more. It all came down to respect. And every day for 55 years that he had been working in the business, he has done his utmost to live this culture, and it shows.

Now that is a fantastic story of an old business that lives to the edict of 'Someone has to be the most expensive, why not make it you? But if you *are* going to be the most expensive, you also have to be the best'.

Do you love your customers?

As I've researched this book and travelled around the world, talking to business owners who really are amazing at what they do, this respect for their customers comes up consistently as a major theme. I remember meeting another old butcher in Brisbane at an event I was doing. He was 85 years old, an immigrant from Italy, and he had been a butcher for 70 years, specialising in making sausages. He was telling me about how he was retiring and handing the reins of the business over to his son.

It was a funny story. The old man told me how his son, who was 65 at the time I might add, wanted to make changes. He wanted to put pepper in one of the salamis that had never had pepper. The old man looked at me, winked, and said, 'Kids, what cha gonna do?' We shared a laugh and I was filled with admiration for this incredible man. I asked him what his secret to success was. He said every single thing he has ever made, he makes it as if it is for his wife, the love of his life. And his customers knew that. They felt the love that he put into everything his hands touched.

If you want to be the best, you have to not only have respect for your customers, I think you have to love your customers. Now I'm not talking romantic love of course, but I'm talking a much deeper and more honest feeling for them than just seeing them as a transaction. They need to know that we respect them, we appreciate them, we value them and they mean a great deal to us.

I will do anything for my customers. And I pretty much have. In this process of charging what you are worth, it's a good idea to think long and hard about your attitude towards your customers. Is it as good as it should be? Is it as respectful as it should be? Do you love them, and if you do, how do you show it?

My values guide how I like to treat everyone, but I always follow this for how I treat my customers:

1. Treat every single customer with respect, ALWAYS.

2. Make every interaction count.

3. Do what others won't.

4. Be there for my customers in good times and bad.

5. When I make a mistake, put my hand up and own it.

6. Always act with absolute integrity.

7. Be strong enough to have hard conversations with my customers.

Every interaction is important when it comes to our customers and every interaction is an opportunity. If we look at our customers as nothing more than a source of income, it shows. They know it, you know it – and the writing is on the wall. Things will not end well. Likewise when they are loved, respected, appreciated and valued, they know it. They will stay supporting you forever if you just keep honouring them and treating them respectfully. There is so much more I would love to say about this, but I'll save it for another book somewhere down the line I think.

28

The transition from simply doing transactions to creating experiences

Transactions have little value, experiences can be priceless. Create experiences.

How to capitalise on the power of business-to-consumer experiences

I was asked to facilitate a session at a conference for about 300 independent sporting goods wholesalers in Melbourne. This was basically a group of independent sports store owners who had banded together as a buying and marketing group. On this particular day, there was quite a lot of excitement, and at the same time a lot of angst.

These retailers were struggling. Times were tough. People could go online and buy what they were selling, particularly sporting shoes, cheaper than they could sell them. In some instances people could buy these shoes cheaper than the retailers could buy them, which was clearly problematic. Addressing this was a big part of the event, and to make it interesting, the CEOs from all the major sporting goods manufacturers were there for a panel – these were the very companies that were selling the products online at cheaper prices. As you can imagine, there was an air of anger in the room.

I was the facilitator of this session, and we had the regional CEOs or equivalent of every major brand, including Nike, Reebok, Adidas and Puma. Just as we were about to start, one of the CEOs

125

asked me if he could say something. So, I moved away from the lectern and let him speak.

He immediately addressed the elephant in the room. He said words to the effect of:

> I know you are all upset by the state of play with the online retail situation, but the reality is that we are not going to stop selling shoes online because we have to do it. Online sales are a huge part of our business, and to stop selling, or to change the price point, would be suicide, because our competitors won't stop. It's not their fault; they are caught in the same position as us.

> So if we are going to spend the next few hours arguing backwards and forwards about the need for us to stop selling our shoes online, this entire session will be a waste of everyone's time. I respectfully suggest that we try a more pragmatic approach.

> One of the challenges you have as retailers is that people can come into your stores, try on a pair of shoes and then go home, find them online and buy them at a substantial discount. Why wouldn't they?

> The real problem here is that the instore experience is not appealing enough to override buying them online. Most of the time, people going into sporting stores are served by a teenager, who has little training, and is only able to ask rudimentary questions about size and colour. You have to make the instore experience so good that your customers will want to buy your shoes right there.

> Remember also, that buying shoes online means delayed gratification, not something people are good with today. It also means that they might end up with the wrong shoes, they could get lost in the mail, they don't fit as well, or any other potential issue that comes with buying online.

> If we spend the next few hours coming up with smart ideas to create extraordinary instore experiences, to the point where price is no longer the issue, your businesses will benefit in so many ways. Now we have the opportunity to work together to make this happen. Let's put our collective minds and resources together.

Lastly, if you want proof of this concept, look at Athlete's Foot. They are the most expensive sports shoe retailer in the country and the most successful. Why? Because they have mastered the art of the instore experience. And they have been doing it for almost 40 years.

My point is very simple: we have to try to create experiences with our promotions, our packaging and our products. We know that our customers don't want transactions, they want experiences and it's our job to give this to them.

This concept is one that I've been very aware of over the past 10 years. It's becoming increasingly important, to the point where I think it's an essential element in business success. The introduction to our event that this CEO gave cemented my thinking and very succinctly explained the reality of the situation. Since then, I've spoken about the importance of moving from transactions to experiences in every corner of the world – from the US to Iran, from Japan to England. People get it, but they struggle with how to do it.

One of the single most important aspects of being able to charge what we are worth is to look at every single touchpoint where we connect in some way with our customers and look for ways to make that experience as distinctive and as memorable as we possibly can. The idea is to surprise our customers, because we are so often left incredibly underwhelmed with our buying experiences.

If I ask people to list their touchpoints, they normally come up with about ten. But that's barely getting started. How about we do this as an exercise – let's work out the touchpoints for a trip to a dentist:

Pre-appointment

- The online experience. Was the site easy to find? Was it easy to use? Could I book online? Was it easy to book online? Was the booking system logical? Was it engaging?

- Was I sent reminders in a way that suited me?

- If I called them, how was the experience? Was I put on hold for a long time? Was the staff member friendly? Were they efficient?

- Could I easily find the location online before visiting?

Visit

- Was it easy to find?

- Was it easy and safe to park?

- Was it well-lit if I was visiting at night?

- What did the front of the business look like?

- Was it clean?

- Did it look fresh and professional or old and tired?

- How was the greeting when I walked in?

- Did the clinic look clean and professional?

- How did it smell?

- How was the ambient noise?

- Was it comfortable to wait?

- What distractions were there in the waiting-room?

- How were the toilets?

- Were the staff engaging or did they ignore me?

- Were they well presented?

- Were they professional?

- Were they reassuring?

- Was I kept informed at every stage about what was going to happen and when?

Moving into the treatment room

- Was I escorted in?

- What did I see along the way?

- Did the nurse introduce themselves?
- Did the dentist introduce themselves?
- How did the chair feel?
- What was the temperature like in the room?
- How did the dental staff interact with me?
- How well informed was I about what was going to happen?
- Were my concerns listened to?
- Was I comfortable?
- How was the treatment?
- Did it hurt?
- Did the dental team talk as if I wasn't in the room?
- Was everything explained clearly to me?
- How was the farewell by the dental team?
- Did I feel like a person or a number?
- Overall, how was the treatment?

Finishing the appointment

- Was my account prepared quickly?
- Did they offer a range of payment options?
- Was I able to pay quickly?
- Was the bill more, less or about what I expected?
- Was I thanked for my business?
- Was the next course of action made clear?

Post-appointment

- Did the dentist or their team follow up to see if I was OK?
- Did I get any further follow-up material or advice that I was promised?

- Would I go back to this dentist?

- Was I sent a reminder for my next appointment?

There are in fact lots of others, but I just closed my eyes and visualised a trip to the dentist. And I'm sure that anyone reading this who has done work on touchpoints understands it's a simple concept to identify them, but to turn as many as possible into great experiences is a little harder.

My advice is to look at each touchpoint – or as I like to call them, 'experience moments' – and assign a value: high, medium or low. High experience values are things like the first greeting, getting taken to the treatment room, meeting the dentist, the actual treatment, getting the bill and so on. Medium value means important but not deal breakers – so, the efficiency of the team, the sounds, the distractions in the waiting-room. And the low value are things like the temperature of the water in the water fountain, the number of goldfish in the tank, what's on the TV set into the ceiling as you are getting treated.

Then go back and do whatever you can to make the high-value experiences extraordinary. And I mean *extraordinary*. And slowly (or quickly) work your way through the list. Get this right and you can certainly charge more. Remember that it's the *combined experiences* that help us to form an overall opinion of a business and our attitude towards their pricing and whether or not we will become fans.

Being the best often means creating the best experiences. I've seen so many examples of this that I actually intend to write a book just about this very topic one day. Here's just a few:

- an 'Arctic room' at an outdoor clothing store in Italy that allows potential buyers to try their purchases in freezing conditions before they buy

- a double-decker bus in London fitted with exercise bikes so that people could do a spin class on their way to work

- a mobile wedding chapel that comes to you in America

- rent a crowd for your funeral in Russia

- a smart condom that comes with an app to help measure performance (seriously)
- a pizza registry for weddings
- Japanese fishermen offering wake-up call services (they call while they are out fishing)
- a gym that is only for people 20kg or more overweight (to help avoid feeling embarrassed)
- a Priest on a Scooter, similar to an UBER – need a priest while in Rome, open the app
- 'melon cam' in China so you can watch your melons grow
- adopt a sheep in the US (and then have a jumper made from its wool).

These are just a handful of examples of businesses that are creating an experience for their customers, and believe me, my list of stories like these number into the thousands. Consumers want experiences. We are open to them, we crave them, and we will reward any business that can deliver them. Experiences create emotional connection and dramatically change the way we feel towards a business.

If you're B2B, you need to do this too

What about if you run an enterprise that is business to business? Does the concept of creating experiences still apply? Absofrickinglutely. In many ways it's even more important, but let's just say for now that it's equally important.

Ironically, I get the most pushback when I'm talking about this topic from business-to-business operations. They come up with all the reasons why it's all about the products and the market and the relationships and the price, all of which certainly need to be considered. But to miss the opportunity of creating experiences for our customers when we are running a business-to-business organisation is a missed opportunity, and a risky one. Because as soon as someone else comes along, selling the same things as you, for around the same price, with the same level of service, but a much better overall experience – you're in trouble, regardless of how long you have been doing business together.

An even bigger strategy is to look at all of your customers' pain points when it comes to buying from you (think about their frustrations, irritations and common sticking points), and figure out how to turn these into your competitive advantage. Think about this for a second. If people always complain about one aspect of your industry – for example, the price of items in mini bars in hotels around the world – imagine if you can make that a competitive advantage for your hotel by making the mini bar free of charge. That's exactly what a very successful hotel in Melbourne does: the Adelphi. They have mastered the concept of taking pain points that all travellers hate and turning them into competitive advantages.

Our job, when trying to charge what we are worth, is to look long and hard at our business and do everything we can to get rid of transactions and make memorable, distinctive experiences. This takes a certain internal culture, it takes creativity, it takes a hunger to look for these opportunities. It never happens by accident. We need to have deeper and more meaningful conversations with our customers and with our staff. We have to become detective-like in our ability to find experiences and, most importantly, we have to take this concept seriously, not just give it lip service, and think that because we've got a chat bot on our site we've created an amazing experience.

29

The importance of being
prepared to *flearn*

*After 35 years in business, I get up every day realising
how little I know about business and how wary
I am of those who have all the answers.*

nother common characteristic of businesses that I would
consider as being the 'best' at what they do is not that they
are risk adverse, but rather they are prepared to take risks,
get things wrong and learn from this. To use the term that best
describes this concept, they are *'flearners'*. They learn from failing.

Interestingly enough, our customers really are OK if we don't
always get it right, as long as we are trying new things, putting effort
into staying relevant, and coming up with new ideas, new products
and new services for them. And as long as we handle it well when
we do make a mistake.

When you think about it, many of our daily appliances actually
come incomplete. They even come with glitches that we find and
report back for them to fix. Phones are probably the single best
example of this. Our iPhones arrive, and normally within a few
weeks the first of the updates and fixes appear. We have to download
them, figure out the changes, accommodate them – and we
don't really look at this as anything but a temporary inconvenience,
nothing more.

The point is that we have never been more accepting of things not being one hundred percent perfect, as long as what's wrong is fixed quickly and efficiently. In fact, we kind of like being part of the research and development team.

Your business should have fans, not just customers

Now, what does this all mean for our businesses? If we are smart, we will have deep and engaging relationships with our customers, to the point where they are fans. Businesses that are the best at what they do have highly motivated fans, not just customers. Our fans, at whichever level they may be, want to see that we are trying new things often, to the point where we will be penalised for not doing new. And if, from time to time, we try something new that goes wrong, as long as we deal with the issue, learn from it and fix the problem rapidly, we will probably build even stronger connections.

Think about the businesses you buy from that you consider to be the best at what they do – the ones for which you are prepared to pay more for their products and services. How accommodating of them are you? How do you feel when they get it wrong, but they own it?

And that last part is the key. When you fail, *own* it. Tell the story of the failure, what you've learned, and what you're doing about it. Engage your customers; show that you respect them and value them enough to share your mistakes. Being the best means being prepared to *flearn*. If you're not *flearning*, you're probably playing it really safe, and that is not what the modern consumer wants.

30

You have to get out a whole lot more to know what others are doing

The best business ideas rarely, if ever, come from within your business or your industry. We have to identify them elsewhere and adapt them to our needs.

When we are in business it's really easy to become a little self-absorbed and obsessed about our business. And from my experience, it seems like everyone else's business is easier to run, far less complicated, clearly making more money than mine, and generally makes me question my very existence. Of course, this isn't true – there is no such thing as an easy business to run (no matter how much the 'internet millionaires' try to convince us). But aside from all of that, being the best means we've got to become a student of other businesses.

As an author, my advice to people who want to write books is for them to become a student of successful authors. If you want to become successful as a speaker, become a student of successful speakers. If you want to build a business that charges the most, and does it successfully with new customers chasing you all the time, you have to become a student of successful businesses that charge the most and are considered the best. This means getting out a whole lot more.

My advice is to invest time and money studying these businesses. Take a Maserati for a test drive: what was the experience like? What's the car like? Was it the same as test driving a Hyundai? Go into a Tiffany store and see what the experience is like.

The key is we have to learn how to observe other businesses, and I don't know that we are necessarily that good at it.

It's time to take the blinkers off

Most business owners are hyper-vigilant about everything to do with their business, but when they leave their business, their blinkers go on. It's time to take the blinkers off. We can learn something from every single business we go into or shop from online if we become keen observers. We might learn what to do; we might learn what *not* to do.

There is so much we can look for. Look at every touchpoint, every aspect of the business – think about it intellectually, but also think about how it made you feel.

Recently I was having a business dinner at a hotel restaurant in Hobart, Tasmania. The restaurant was really nice, well appointed, with friendly staff and good food. The menu wasn't astonishing, but they used lots of local produce and clearly the chefs were good at preparing meals that represented the region well.

I had to go to the bathroom, and as I entered the first thing I noticed was how clean they were (that tells me a lot about a business, especially a restaurant – if they don't care enough to keep the toilets clean, what does it say about the food?). But there were two things I saw that really created an emotional feeling for me. They used 'Who Gives a Crap' toilet paper and 'Thankyou' handwash. Now both of these products have major social good elements associated with them. Buying them means that someone cares enough to not just buy the generic, cheapest products but rather they care about the environment and the people living on the planet enough to make more considered buying decisions.

I went back to the table and asked everyone the question: 'If I told you this restaurant had "Who Gives a Crap" toilet paper and "Thankyou" hand wash, what message does that send you? And do you feel more positive about the overall experience here?'

The response was absolutely unanimous – everyone's perception changed or was enhanced. Everyone really liked the fact that the restaurant was making considered purchases, and last but not least, everyone felt that the restaurant was good value (even though it was one of the most expensive in Hobart).

Spend a great deal of time studying businesses. I do it face to face, I do it online – I do it however I can. And I learn a great deal. When it comes to those businesses that charge the most, and that thrive year after year, these are the businesses we can learn the most from. Blinkers off, go and buy yourself some expensive stuff (OK, or just pop in for a visit), but learn, learn, learn. Identify that thing or those things that make them special.

31

It's about doing small really well

We think succeeding in business is about the
big things. From my experience, it's so much more
about doing the little things well.

I was doing a road trip a few years back, driving from Cairns
to Brisbane, about 1600kms down the Queensland Coast in
Australia. It's a long trip, and to be honest after the first few hours
of leaving Cairns, there isn't much to see. It's a long, functional
drive, on a road mainly used by business travellers and tourists looking for the Australian experience. The town of Rockhampton is
about half-way, and that's where I decided to stop for the night.

As soon as I pulled up at a big motel, I realised everyone else
seemed to have had the same idea. I found a parking space, went
inside, and managed to get a room at this simple but clean and very
accommodating motel, with great staff and lots of little features that
justified it's 'higher than everyone else's' rates. (I often see the most
expensive business of its kind in a certain area being the one that is
fully booked – not a coincidence methinks.)

I slept well, got up early, had a good breakfast, paid my bill and
carried my bags to the car, feeling well rested and ready for the next
mindless slog of kilometre after kilometre. As I climbed into my car,
I noticed a note on my windscreen. I reached around and noticed
that someone had cleaned my windscreen – all the bugs and road
muck was gone.

The note read:

Thank you for choosing to stay at the Rockhampton Motor Inn. We've taken the liberty of cleaning your windscreen so that the road ahead will be clear and safe. Please come and stay with us again.

Now this simple little gesture had such a big impact on me. I've stayed at many hotels, from very expensive ones to very cheap ones, but I've only ever had one similar experience (a motel in Tasmania gave every guest a small bag of apples and some bottles of water for the trip ahead).

The card and the clean windscreen completely changed my emotional connection with the motel in Rockhampton. It was such a simple yet powerful thing, simply because no one else does it. And as I started to contemplate my stay, I realised that everything the motel did worked – they met and exceeded every one of my expectations. My whole stay was actually very good, but being in a fatigued and road-weary state, I didn't really notice. The simple act of putting a note under the windscreen wiper told me they cared, and upon reflection it showed during my stay.

Small things are a big way to differentiate your business

We often think that winning or losing customers is about the big things we do. But in reality, it's becoming more and more about the small things we do. These are the things that differentiate a business and generally say a lot about that business.

Since my card on the windscreen, I've become a student of small things in businesses. I look for those things that stop me in my tracks and make me take real notice of a business, especially when they are in a crowded space. It's always the little things. Just yesterday, I had some dry cleaning done while I was staying in a hotel and my suit came back with a sprig of lavender pinned to the bag. A very small gesture, but one that had my suit smelling nice, and a sign that whoever owns this business cares. Message received.

Those businesses that proudly wear the moniker of being the best and charge accordingly generally have a team of people who pay attention to the small things. They make the experience associated with the small things exceptional. Add lots of small and wonderful experiences together and you build a reputation and a brand which will have customers clambering to buy what you are selling and pay what you are charging.

32

Being the best is often about the emotion that seeing something of yours creates

The bigger the emotional connection the more you can charge.

Imagine you see a couple at a restaurant, sitting and having a nice romantic dinner. The man pulls out a turquoise-green box with a ribbon around it. For most people, this box is instantly recognisable as a Tiffany box — and with that comes a vast amount of meaning and significance. The Tiffany colour is so easily recognisable — regardless of whether it is on a box, a bag or a magazine advertisement — that the colour says everything. Imagine how wonderful it would be to have a brand so easily recognisable, with very deep and emotive messages conveyed simply by having an easily recognisable colour?

The same applies to many brands. We are all familiar with the Mercedes-Benz logo — it infers quality at a Mercedes-Benz level. Many car brands do the same thing — Ferrari, Lamborghini, the Maserati trident — one look at their logo and all kinds of emotive messages are passed, and it doesn't need to be on the grille of a car.

What about the Nike swoosh? We don't really need any words to tell us to 'just do it'.

It's about making connections

Most successful brands, whether they are big global brands or small local brands, have the ability to create an emotional connection with their audiences. And that's the secret sauce of marketing.

My point here is that these brands, and many other high-end brands, have done something very special: they have all managed to transfer the value associated with their products, the common and consistent features, and the emotion associated with owning them or being given them, and created an emotional connection with their logo. This is to the point where simply seeing the logo says a great deal about whatever it is they are selling, and the level of credibility is established with nothing more than an image.

This is, in many ways, what we all should be aspiring too. But can we do that with our products and services when we don't have the might of a gazillion-dollar marketing budget? Or a hundred-year history of building a global brand? I think we can.

If your business is one where you are the product – meaning people buy products or services from you, probably education-al-type products or services – your personal brand is the same as your Mercedes-Benz logo. And this is a very good reason to really work to build and develop your business brand all the time. If people associate your brand with quality, they will be prepared to pay accordingly for what it is you sell.

When it comes to building a brand for a more traditional style of business, you still have to build your brand, but it has to become known for all the right things before people will pay for the quality you are offering.

The key is – add emotion. This is *your* emotion, meaning tell your story, share more about what got you here, your origin story, what you stand for, your commitment story, your process – let people into your business so they can see the meaning behind what you do. As simple as this sounds, this is what works.

Part VI

DOES THIS CONCEPT REALLY WORK FOR ANY KIND OF BUSINESS IN ANY MARKET?

We have to become masters of zigging
when everyone else is zagging.

Where are you now on your road to becoming the most expensive?

PART I: The BIG why ...

PART II: The world has changed – have you?

PART III: There are many very good reasons to be the most expensive

PART IV: How scared does this idea make you?

PART V: So what does it actually mean to be the best?

PART VI: Does this concept really work for any kind of business in any market?

PART VII: Surely the online world is completely different? Or is it?

PART VIII: Now we are convinced of the reasoning, we need some rules to work with

PART IX: The process we need to follow

PART X: Now it's time to rethink what we say

PART XI: More ways to increase your credibility, trustworthiness and 'buyability'

Part XII: This road is not for the faint of heart

HAVING WORKED WITH BUSINESSES large and small, in virtually every corner of the planet, across most industries imaginable, when I raise the concept of charging what you are really worth, or even more powerfully, stepping up and becoming the most expensive in your industry or in your space, I often get asked the question, 'Does this concept really apply to any kind of business in any market?'

It's a great question, and one that I'm going to answer in this part. To me, the simple answer is 'yes'. And in fact I'm going to explain why being the most expensive is a great strategy to survive in a tough market, when the first response is often to slash prices and run back to the supposed safety of selling on price alone.

I often have people say to me that the idea is good, but it won't possibly work for them: their customers are completely price-driven, or the market will only pay a certain amount. As soon as I hear these arguments starting to flow, it tells me that there is a lot of limited belief thinking and old stories being told.

I spoke about my first business, my dive shop, earlier. How my model was completely price-driven because that was all I knew. When my thinking was challenged on this, everything changed.

A great example of this was the dive equipment I stocked. Basically my entire store was filled with the cheapest equipment I could find. Why? Because that's what the guy I bought the shop from sold. He told me that's what people wanted – it was relatively easy to sell because it was cheap and I could buy more of it because it was cheap. Sounds like a reasonable set of assumptions, right?

The problem was that it was lousy dive equipment. It didn't last very long, it constantly broke down, people complained all the time, the company I bought it from had lousy service and really didn't care. And the biggest problem of all? I made next to nothing every time I sold this equipment because the price was so low.

An equipment sales rep from a high-end company became a friend of mine. One day he dropped by for a coffee, knowing that I probably wasn't going to buy anything from him. We started chatting and I told him about my woes with this gear. He looked me in the eye and – with a befuddled look – asked me why on earth I kept selling this cheap stuff. My only answer was that it was what my customers wanted – but he called me on this: 'Is it *really* what they want or have you become lazy at selling?' Then he asked a big question: 'Do *you* use that cheap brand as an instructor?' And of course I didn't; I used the top-of-the-line, most expensive equipment. Why? Because my life depended on it. And at that moment I got it.

I ordered some of his top-end equipment then and there. I was really worried; it cost a fortune and I'd just done my big store renovation, so I was broke. He offered to teach me how to sell a better type of equipment – and he put his sales skills to the test with the next customer to walk through the door.

His sales approach was simple. The customer was looking to buy some SCUBA gear, but they made it very clear that they were on a tight budget. My sales rep friend brought over two sets of equipment to show the customer, the cheap gear and the top-of-the-line gear. His sales pitch was simple: 'This set is the cheapest on the market, and this set is the best on the market. I use the best because my life depends on it. Which set would you like?'

That was it. The customer pulled out a credit card, bought a $4000 set of equipment versus a $1500 set of equipment. And he walked out really happy.

I was flabbergasted. I'd never come close to selling an expensive set of gear like that, and I honestly didn't think anyone, other than a professional diver, would ever spend that much. It was a very big moment for me. From that day on I never sold one of the cheap sets of gear ever again. Now, I'm not saying that I sold every customer a set of high-end gear; some people didn't buy and they would have gone off and bought the cheap gear somewhere else. But in my shop, we never, ever sold cheap gear again. And it was transformational in every way.

So what changed? Well, my customer base was changing anyway, but I now attracted people looking for quality gear. In fact, we built our reputation on it. I made far more money, because the gear I now sold had a much higher profit margin. And because it was such good quality, it rarely broke down, and if it did the company replaced it with no questions asked. This was incorporated into our sales spiel. And our reputation grew because our service was extraordinary.

Last but not least, my customers stood a little taller in this gear, because of the status associated with this high-quality brand. People noticed. And I often heard them on dive trips where we would be with divers from other clubs, getting asked why they used such high-end, expensive gear, and they would literally say word-for-word my sales spiel. I loved these moments. Everyone wins.

Next, I bought this expensive gear to use in my SCUBA school – this was unheard of. But I wanted to put my money where my mouth was. So my students saw that we used the best gear available in our training classes – what message did that send when everyone else was using cheap and nasty equipment? We could charge far more for our SCUBA classes as a result.

I'm sure you can see the clear moral to this story. I was stuck in an old story, believing two things: that my customers wanted cheap dive equipment, and that this was the only equipment I could possibly sell. You get the point, I'm sure.

Even in the toughest of times, in the toughest of markets, there is always that one business that seems to be thriving, and they are the most expensive. They are bucking the trend, going against the tide, zigging when everyone else is zagging. And that's why this concept is so powerful. Business success is not about going with the flow in the modern world we live in. It's about being brave enough to do the exact opposite. Those businesses that possess this courage get rewarded.

33

It's the perfect time to be the best

We have never been as prepared to
pay for quality as we are today.

Without a doubt, the reason this concept of being the most expensive can work now more than ever is the combination of a number of converging trends around the world, mostly revolving around changing consumer patterns and the rise of communication opportunities. In other words, there are more people prepared to buy high-quality products and services, and it's really easy for them to find these products and services.

So when the question is asked, 'Will this concept work for any business in any market?', I honestly believe it will. And, in fact, I believe it more every day as I spend time researching the topic and looking for businesses around the world that continue to prove the idea. While the majority of businesses in a market sector are fighting it out in the cheap end of town, those that are able to deliver a higher level product or service tend to have far fewer competitors.

Let's talk for a few minutes about communication. We are living in the 'Age of the Entrepreneur' without a doubt, and one of the reasons we have become so entrepreneurial is our ability to communicate.

Every single day I spend time researching businesses online. I look for weird and unusual business ideas, innovative thinking, inventions, trends, new products and services – and time and time again, I find them and in most instances I could buy something from them right then and there on my laptop. And it doesn't matter where in the world they are. People doing smart things get found online because there is a giant appetite from people who want to know more.

I watched a television show about Austin Texas and a famous BBQ restaurant, Franklin BBQ, was featured. I've heard about this place and been amazed by just how successful it actually is. Now the kicker. People will line up for two or three hours to get into this restaurant to buy a tray of BBQ meat and sit and eat it in basically a cafeteria setting. Seriously? They start lining up hours before it opens – the line goes around the block, people bring chairs, eskis, work on their laptops, content to wait to get this food. Is it cheap? Is that what draws people in? Absolutely not. It's incredible quality. But could it possibly be *that* good?

This restaurant is featured on every travel show that goes to Austin (I've seen it on seven shows with audiences as high as 130 million people). Can you imagine that kind of exposure? Am I going there next time I go to Austin? You bet!

Fascinating stories about people doing smart things

We love hearing fascinating stories about people doing smart things. And from my experience, smart things generally happen where businesses are the best at what they do. Where creativity flourishes and where there is an incredible commitment to being the best. Would you like a business where people are prepared to line up for hours because what you make or sell is so damn good?

My point here is that word of mouth, and even more impor- tantly word of mouse, is significant today. It always has been, but now it's on steroids. Food is one space where this is so incredibly relevant.

I live in Melbourne, Australia, one of the great food cities of the world. I see so many examples of 'someone has to be the most expensive, why not make it you? But if you *are* going to be the most expensive, you also have to be the best'. From extraordinary croissants and bread to incredible delis and markets. The world is in love with everything food, and when you combine quality and with what others consider to be a little crazy, and a wonderful commitment to being the best, amazing things can happen.

If you do great things, if you really aspire to be the best at what you do, not only can you charge exactly what you are worth because the right people will find you, but you will find you have an army of sales reps who will tell the world why they should be buying what you sell.

34

Being the most expensive is actually the best way to survive in a tough market

There are two types of business:
those that have had tough times and
those that are going to have tough times.

There are two types of businesses out there: those that have had tough times financially and those that are going to have tough times financially – there are no exceptions to this. Surviving these tough times is the key.

I have gone to great lengths to point out the challenges of having a price-driven strategy for any business, and the benefits of actually charging what you are worth. But one of the biggest benefits I'd like to spend some time discussing is the concept that being the most expensive is actually the best way to survive in a tough market.

Price-driven businesses are usually the first to go

The reality is that price-driven or cheap businesses are generally the first to go when we have to tighten our belts. They simply lack the resources to keep going; they often don't have the cash reserves, and their customers, who are the cheap customers, also start to feel the crunch sooner so they stop spending faster. All in all, it leads to disaster. I've seen it through many economic downturns, time and time again. As I write this in the midst of the COVID-19 pandemic, it's sadly being illustrated in incredible numbers, with so many businesses going bust so fast that it shows the real depth of this issue.

Businesses that tend to charge what they are worth and that are the most expensive (and to me this means they are the best at what they do) have the potential to be far more profitable, and hence they are stable and able to better ride out rough economic conditions. But when you think about it, so are their customers. If your customers are prepared to pay for quality, they are more likely to be more affluent and more able to weather economic challenges.

Now, I know I'm making a few generalisations here. Often when tough times hit the first things to go are the flash cars, the jet skis and all other toys. I'm not really talking about those kinds of customers. I'm talking about the people with a more secure and less erratic wealth base. And there are plenty of them around.

Again, from the work I do globally, and the research I've conducted, the more profitable the business, the more likely it is to survive. And we make our businesses more profitable by making sure we have a good margin. The best way to do this is to offer excellent products and services at the right price, making this a very smart and practical strategy for getting through the inevitable tough times.

35

There is always a reason why this concept won't work – but is it fact or fiction?

It's amazing how when the need gets urgent enough, all of the things that were once impossible now miraculously become not only possible but essential.

I have a friend who specialises in starting real estate businesses at the bottom of the market. He waits until a particular town that he likes is in the midst of a real estate crash, and when it seems to be at it's worst, he goes in, opens his doors and charges what he is worth, easily being the most expensive. He's done this numerous times, selling out for millions when the market peaks. He bucks the trends and zigs when everyone else is zagging.

So, what is his philosophy and strategy? It's simple and genius. When the market is at its worst, it doesn't mean people aren't buying or selling, it means that fewer people are buying and selling. And prices for properties fluctuate accordingly.

Typically at this time, most other real estate agents are sitting around crying into their coffee, saying things like 'no one is buying or selling – we have to ride it out'. While they are riding it out and convincing themselves that no one is buying or selling, keeping the myth alive, my friend goes in, full of energy and passion, finds the best salespeople in town, hires them (they are easy to find because they are sick and tired of the doom-and-gloom talk), he fires them up and they go out actively looking for new customers. They don't buy into the rhetoric of what is or isn't going on. They know there are always people wanting to buy and people wanting to sell – they just have to find them.

They also know that when everyone is filled with doom and gloom and the apathy has set in, their greatest opportunity is to be the exact opposite. Be energetic, be smart, be proactive, really deliver extraordinary service, go the extra mile – and charge accordingly. All the other agents slash their prices during these tough times; my friend is easily the most expensive in town. And who do you think ends up very quickly being the top agent sales-wise during the tough times? You guessed it. And if he is kicking butt in the tough times, you can imagine what his business is like in the good times, right?

The bottom line: the customers are still there. We know people always want to buy and sell property, but finding the right people is often about our attitude, how we position ourselves, how we market, the experience we deliver and the ability to zig when everyone else is zagging. We need to be smarter, more agile and able to adapt, and – a word I've used often – courageous.

A few years back I needed to buy a new car. I had lent my car to a friend, he had an accident and wrote it off. He was OK, even though I wanted to kill him. At the time the idea of buying a new car was really more of a pain for me than anything else. So I set out on a Saturday morning, dressing down to look cheap, and I started to visit every car dealer on the strip.

I wandered around cars in the lots, dressed in my daggy tee-shirt and shorts. I had about $40,000 to spend that day. I stood around waiting. No one came to speak to me. If I went inside I might have been given a brochure, but the sales staff were hopeless. I went to six dealers in a row – and not a single sales rep made an effort to sell me a car.

Now, the real irony of this was the front cover of the newspaper that Saturday had the lead story 'NEW CAR MARKET WORST IT'S BEEN FOR 10 YEARS'. How ironic. I'm trying to give my money away and no one would come and take it. Till I got to the seventh dealer.

The sales manager here was fantastic. He walked up to me, shook my hand, looked me up and down a little but didn't let his thoughts out. He took me to his office; we spent ages talking about what I needed a car for. Then he took me straight to the car he recommended. It cost $80,000, which was double my budget and I spent it gladly. I bought it on the spot. That's how good the experience was and the actual vehicle he recommended was. Which I might add, is the car I still drive, 12 years later.

It's time to explore your thinking

So back to the title for this chapter: 'There is always a reason why this concept won't work – but is it fact or fiction?' When we find that we are saying things like, 'this is a cute idea but it won't work for us', we really need to stop and explore that thinking. What is it based on? I think it therefore it is? Or is it simply what everyone else in the industry is saying so that makes it true? Or is what we are reading in the local newspaper? Telling us how tough times are?

Fact or fiction?

When it comes to the concept of charging what we are worth, or being the most expensive, we have to deal with facts not fiction.

This particular point is really interesting and timely. As I finish this book we are bang in the midst of COVID-19 and all that it's entailed. We have had to deal with social isolation, business hibernation, closed businesses, no travel – all kinds of things we never imagined happening. What's been fascinating for me is all the things that we pre-COVID-19 thought unimaginable – never going to happen, impossible – and then suddenly, they happened. Businesses likewise had to do the same – evolve on the spot, come up with new business models overnight, modify their products and services like crazy – or just roll over and die.

In many ways it was like business evolution was put in a time machine and taken forward ten years. Everything happened so fast, but people asked 'what if' far more because they didn't have a choice. Choices sometimes make us lazy. Make us stick with the status quo as opposed to getting really uncomfortable and trying something completely new.

One line I've heard surprisingly often driving COVID-19 in the small business space has been: 'I've completely changed my business model … and I wish I'd done this 10 years ago.'

Kind of makes you wonder, doesn't it?

Part VII

SURELY THE ONLINE WORLD IS COMPLETELY DIFFERENT? OR IS IT?

In a world of homogenised online businesses, this is a big opportunity.

Where are you now on your road to becoming the most expensive?

PART I: The BIG why ...

PART II: The world has changed – have you?

PART III: There are many very good reasons to be the most expensive

PART IV: How scared does this idea make you?

PART V: So what does it actually mean to be the best?

PART VI: Does this concept really work for any kind of business in any market?

PART VII: Surely the online world is completely different? Or is it?

PART VIII: Now we are convinced of the reasoning, we need some rules to work with

PART IX: The process we need to follow

PART X: Now it's time to rethink what we say

PART XI: More ways to increase your credibility, trustworthiness and 'buyability'

Part XII: This road is not for the faint of heart

I THINK THE ANSWER to this question is that there *are* differences doing business online but it isn't *completely* different. The concept of what I'm suggesting in this book about charging what you are worth certainly applies to the online world as much as a bricks-and-mortar business, but it is a little harder because we have fewer touchpoints to enhance the overall customer experience. This means that the touchpoints we have really need to be pretty darn exceptional.

We also need to consider the fact that as consumers we are becoming much more online savvy. Most people would have some experience of buying a product or service online, and most of us subscribe to things like Netflix or Apple Music. Millions of us buy books online regularly. We even go online to order dinner, thanks to apps like Uber Eats and Deliveroo.

Many of these purchases were kind of novelties when we started to buy online, but now we are more sophisticated, we've had plenty of bad experiences, and our expectations are generally quite low. To me, that represents great opportunity.

Our expectations and our experiences with making purchases online varies dramatically. Think about your own online buying habits. You have things you buy regularly, maybe on a subscription basis, that you are happy to pay for each month because you get good value out of the purchase. Other things you buy regularly but you ask yourself often if you should keep buying it. And last but not least, the things you buy once and swear that you'll never buy again.

Add to this the fact that two businesses can sell the same product – one delivers an excellent experience, the other is lousy from the start all the way to the finish. The product is exactly the same, but one business gets it and the other doesn't. This shows the importance of our online systems, mechanisms and fulfilment aspects.

If we add each of these musings together, I think we come back to the same point. When it comes to the online world, we most certainly have the same opportunity as we do with a bricks-and-mortar business. Someone has to be the most expensive, online as much as offline. You can be that business, but you have to be really good at delivering, and I mean *every aspect* of delivering, not just the package in the post.

Spend a few minutes reflecting once again on your online purchases. Who do you buy from regularly and why? How often do you buy online only to be left feeling very underwhelmed by the experience? How often are you blown away by the experience?

The key to our success in the online world is to learn from those who are very good at it, specifically selling high-price, high-value products and services. The online world caters for the price-conscious customer wonderfully well already. It's only now that the quality-focused consumer is starting to get their needs and expectations met. And that spells opportunity to me.

36

Are online businesses any different?

When we sell online we have to
work harder to show quality.

This is an important discussion to have, especially in light of
the fact that so many businesses are starting in the online
space, or moving to an online-only retail presence. Can the
principle of charging what you are worth – or even better, being
the most expensive – apply to the online space?

I certainly think it can, and there is evidence to support that,
but, and it is a big but, the challenge is that we have fewer significant
touchpoints to show our value and the aspects of what makes us the
best at what we do. So we have two options: use our bricks-and-
mortar presence to act as a gateway to get customers to buy online,
or alternatively, make the online experience so good, so compelling
and so easy that our customers are happy to buy online from day one.

Why I pay $35 for deodorant

To illustrate option one, I buy household cleaning products, dog wash
and even human wash and smell-good-type stuff from a brand called
Aesop. This is a luxury Australian brand now owned by a Brazilian
company. Their in-store is experience is good, very personal and
efficient, and the stores themselves are simply but beautifully fitted
out. Since becoming a customer I don't need to go to the store to

buy; I'm happy to buy their products online, simply because I know what I'm going to get. This is crucial – the risk is removed.

Add to this the fact that when you buy from Aesop their online store is very easy to use. It reflects their overall retail experience: simple, to the point, high quality at a higher price. Your order arrives promptly and it is very well packaged, so no risk of leakage or breakage.

For this, I pay $35 for an Aesop deodorant compared to a deodorant from the shelves of a large grocery store that I can buy for $5. Is it worth it? To me? Absolutely. To many others? Absolutely. Probably to the majority – no way. But that's OK, because Aesop don't want every customer in the market for deodorant, they want *their* customers. The instore and the online experiences align – a great customer experience and very good quality product.

My point here is that I'm not sure if I would have become an Aesop customer if I didn't have a chance to buy their products in store first. I started buying from their retail stores and transitioned to buying online. This is a common transition, and if the retailer can make the online experience comparable to the instore experience it will probably work. (Sadly, it rarely is.) And if the retailer can make the online experience really good, they can certainly charge more.

The second option, one where we have to create an exceptional online experience from the start to get our quality customers, is a biggie, and to be honest, one that seems to challenge a lot of businesses. I think this is mainly because they are not face-to-face with customers – this leads to service issues because of a lack of direct feedback. We can all relate to the frustration of trying to buy something from a company's website only to give up 20 minutes later. It's like they have purposely gone out of their way to make it ridiculously complicated.

Or even worse, we make the purchase and it takes an extremely long amount of time to turn up (if in fact it does turn up). And often when it does turn up, its fails to meet any of our expectations, and we have to start the process of either sending it back and trying to get a refund or just writing it off as an online learning experience.

So what does all of this translate to for doing business online? In my opinion, it's easier to transition a customer to our online world if they buy our products and services offline and get to experience the quality of what we do. If we are purely online, then we need to focus on:

1. Our website needs to be really smart and totally customer-friendly (get customers involved in the design and initial testing of the site).

2. We need a visit to our site to be compelling; it needs to be an experience. This means great images, engaging storytelling, video content, testimonials – the secret sauce that makes us different really needs to be clear.

3. We need to make it incredibly easy for people to buy our products and services.

4. Our packaging and delivery of these products and services needs to be exceptional.

5. We have to deliver fast.

6. Opening the package needs to be an experience that we love.

7. The quality of what the customer receives has to meet their expectations, and ideally exceed them.

8. We need to be able to do this time and time again – with the same high level of everything, delivered consistently.

9. We need to evolve the online experience as our customers evolve.

10. We need to constantly be asking better questions – how can we constantly make this easier, faster and a better experience for our customers?

Sounds like a lot, but is it really? If we can't do the above, maybe we shouldn't be in the online business.

37

Understanding why people buy online is the place to start – and not everyone is the same

The key to capturing a market is to know the market.
It's surprisingly simple, yet so often overlooked.

It's not just about the price

I'm sure that for a lot of people the main reason they started buying online was because of price, but now there's much more to it. Now I'm finding that even with my own online shopping habits, there are a few reasons why I buy from trusted businesses, and price is not really at the top of the list.

Let's have a look at why we buy online these days.

To save time

If I have a business I like to buy from, and I know and trust the products, I'll gladly buy their products online rather than visiting their shop. To me this is all about convenience. My time is precious, and to drive to a specific store to buy an item that I buy regularly is a waste of time when I can order it online and have it delivered to my door. Convenience is a very big factor for shopping online, and it's becoming increasingly important as we all get busier.

I can shop when it suits me

Buying online is convenient because we can shop at any time. In a world that's becoming increasingly busy, convenience is becoming far more important for many people than price. I'm happy to pay a premium for convenience, but generally you don't have to.

It's the easiest option for buying a product that's hard to get your hands on

I love Tasmania. I spend a lot of time there. I have been a regular visitor for well over 35 years. In fact, one of my earliest entrepreneurial forays was selling encyclopaedias door to door throughout Tasmania (and if you want to learn how to sell, that's the ultimate baptism of fire). There are certain specific products I've discovered in Tasmania over the years; one is honey and the other is olive oil. Both come from specialist producers and both are expensive.

It's really hard to find other people who sell these two products produced like this, so it's actually much easier for me to buy them directly from the producers via their websites and have the products shipped to me. Why do I do this? Simply because of the quality of these products.

We love a world of choice

Clearly it's much easier to list a pile of products or services online than it is in a bricks-and-mortar retail store. The sheer logistics of managing stock becomes much easier for most online outlets, as there is a little more leeway when it comes to dispatching the goods. When we buy in a shop, we expect to leave with the product; when we buy online, once the order is made, we know it will be winging its way towards us shortly. So, online sellers are generally able to have bigger ranges and that means more choice for us the consumer.

And of course for many products and services, price is still a factor

Many of us use online shopping to compare prices for everything from shoes to hotel accommodation to new cars. I completely understand that price is a consideration, but my point here is that just as with offline businesses, if people are only buying from you because you're the cheapest, there are certainly going to be issues with long-term success, profitability and longevity of your business.

★ ★ ★

Ideally you need to know why people want to buy your products and services online – and therefore what their most important purchasing considerations are. The principles I've been talking about throughout this book apply: if you offer a high-quality product or service, market it well and really deliver outstanding service and experiences with shipping and delivery, I believe you can charge what you are worth, and even apply the 'someone has to be the most expensive' model to your online business.

The problem is that few online experiences live up to our expectations, especially when buying from overseas. Have you ever made that late-night mistake of buying something that comes up in your Facebook feed – something that looks like a good idea at the time, but deep down, you start worrying about whether or not it will live up to your expectations the minute you press the final 'BUY NOW' button?

More about this in the next chapter, but for now, we need to know that just like there are price-driven customers and value-driven customers offline, they exist in the online world as well. We need to know which ones we want and how we are going to attract them and meet their expectations.

38

How does the 'experience' influence online prices?

When it comes to online, we have to
work harder to create the experience.

ight about now I'm pretty certain that you've picked up
on my ongoing and constant reference to the importance
of 'customer experience' when it comes to charging what
you are worth. A great experience goes a long way to achieving
that. And generally, the business that is the absolute best at what
they do, and they are the most expensive, will offer a very good
customer experience.

When we're dealing with customers face to face, there is more
pressure to deliver great service (but of course that doesn't mean we
always get it – some businesses simply have no flaming idea). But
when we are selling online, there is a certain distance from the customer that makes it less personal, and so it's far easier for the level of
service to drop dramatically. You can't let that happen if you want to
charge more. In fact, you have to be looking for ways to make *every*
experience better, not just face-to-face experiences.

Make your online experience the best it can be

How can you make your online experience the best it can be so that you can charge accordingly? Here are just a few simple ideas that, to me, will definitely create a better experience:

- Make it personal – add a handwritten note of some kind to go with every purchase. It takes time but it makes a huge impact. Look for ways to make the sale more personal. Get creative. Reach out and ask some of your existing customers what they would like. And while you're at it, ask them what they *don't* like about your online service.

- Have fun with your confirmation message. Customise the confirmation email. Add a link to a thank-you video page. Offer something unexpected that will surprise the customer.

- Add a product sample – the company I buy my honey from in Tasmania always includes a sample of another product of theirs which, while I don't always buy, I do always try, and I really appreciate that they do this.

- Invest in quality packaging – protect the items that are being shipped, and make opening the package a good experience for the customer.

- Have some fun – be playful with your packaging, if it's appropriate. Make your packaging distinct – we all know the Amazon smile on packages, right? I've seen businesses that have produced fun stickers, suggestions for reusing the box, quotes from other customers, inspirational quotes, recipes, maps, stories printed on wrapping paper about the people behind the product, and many other wonderful things.

- Be considered with your packaging. I bought a book online recently, and when it arrived there was so much packaging for this one book that I felt guilty. It was so over the top and wasteful in a time when we are all trying to be far more considered about the environment.

- Showcase more about your business than just the products and services you sell. Show other aspects of production and delivery. I love that UPS in America has a Facebook page set-up which showcases the pets their drivers meet along the way (just search Facebook for 'UPS dogs'). It's really nice, sends a warm message, and has 1.8 million people following the page. That's much more than just delivering packages.

Remember, experience equals value. The better the experience for the customer, the more they will value the purchase and the more you can charge. It's a simple equation, yet one that very few businesses get right – and therein lies the opportunity for you and for me.

39

Buy stuff online and start to find businesses who do it really well and learn from them

If you don't buy online you probably won't succeed at selling online.

I strongly recommend you become a student of other businesses, in this case those that sell online. Spend some money, buy some things, get a feel for those that are doing it really well and those that are hopeless. It's kind of interesting to see just how different the online experience can be.

Questions to ask with every online purchase

What do we want to learn? I think there are lots of things we can learn to help us improve our own overall online experience, regardless of what we sell. Questions to ask with every online purchase include:

- Why did I buy this particular product?

- Did I shop around for price?

- If I was considering buying a product from several sites, how did I finally decide which one to make the purchase from?

- How easy was it to get the information I needed to make a decision?

- How easy was it to actually buy the item? (So many businesses seem to go out of their way to make buying overly complicated.)

- What was the confirmation of the sale like?

- How long did it take for the item to arrive? Was that better than expected, about what I expected, or worse?

- How was the packaging?

- How was the experience of opening the package?

- Overall, what did I learn from this acquisition?

All too often we are living and running our businesses in a little bubble. I'm a giant fan of looking at how other businesses do what they do and what I can learn from them. Sometimes I get to learn what *not* to do, other times I pick up pure gold, simply because I took the time to look and learn as opposed to going through life with my blinkers on. Interestingly enough, I find I learn a great deal more from the smaller, quiet achievers than the loud, yelling, 'I've got all of the answers' entrepreneurs and coaches and experts.

But I digress. Buy stuff online, learn from the experience. I actually think that if you don't buy online, you probably shouldn't be selling online and, in all reality, you're far less likely to be successful at it.

40

We need to stay constantly across the dynamics of the online world

Learn, learn, learn.

Just as I've suggested buying things online to really get a feel for how other quality businesses manage the customer experience side of things, I think it's vitally important for those with the aspiration of charging more for what they do to stay across the dynamics of the online world.

Tech is obviously changing daily. There are always new platforms, tools and resources that we can buy and incorporate into our online offering. But we don't tend to stumble across these things unless we are looking for them.

If you want to be the best, expect only the best from your suppliers

At the same time, you need to be working with suppliers who are right at the coalface of online selling and tech. You want to work with a web development company that's coming to you with ideas to make the experience better all the time. And from my experience, these kinds of developers are hard to find.

Often web developers seem to specialise in telling you the things you can't do with a site. When I hear this, I translate it as 'they can't do it'. Don't be afraid of finding a web developer who gets your drive and ambition to be the best at what you do and who will help you get there. Ideally, find the web developer who is the best at what they do.

Sure, it's going to cost you more, but another one of the changes that starts to happen when you are the most expensive is you start to respect – and expect – quality in your suppliers. We not only start to value ourselves more, we start to value others, and we are more inclined to pay for quality. And that's when we know we are on the right path. For example, the best restaurants, and the most expensive restaurants, pride themselves on using only the best ingredients available, provided by the best producers.

Stay across the online world. Think about your own buying habits and the evolution of the businesses you buy from online. Learn, learn, learn.

Part VIII

NOW WE ARE CONVINCED OF THE REASONING, WE NEED SOME RULES TO WORK WITH

If you don't know the rules,
it's hard to play the game let alone win.

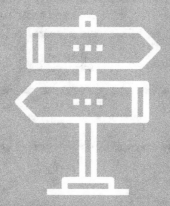

Where are you now on your road to becoming the most expensive?

PART I: The BIG why ...

PART II: The world has changed — have you?

PART III: There are many very good reasons to be the most expensive

PART IV: How scared does this idea make you?

PART V: So what does it actually mean to be the best?

PART VI: Does this concept really work for any kind of business in any market?

PART VII: Surely the online world is completely different? Or is it?

PART VIII: Now we are convinced of the reasoning, we need some rules to work with

PART IX: The process we need to follow

PART X: Now it's time to rethink what we say

PART XI: More ways to increase your credibility, trustworthiness and 'buyability'

Part XII: This road is not for the faint of heart

THESE 12 RULES that absolutely have to be adhered to so we can successfully transition into charging what we are worth, and ideally becoming the most expensive, provide us with some parameters to work with. They are our compliance guidelines, and they are vitally important.

Hopefully by now I've well and truly convinced you about why being the most expensive is a smart business move. But simply doubling your prices and hoping for the best is not really what I would call a strategy – in fact, I'd suggest it's a business suicide mission.

Just as most of us built our poverty mentality up over years, it's unlikely we will get rid of it overnight. Most of the time, we simply get sick and tired enough of never actually making any money so we *finally* take action – or we don't, choosing instead to get old and poor.

To make the transition into being the most expensive we need two things:

- We need a set of guiding principles or, dare I say, some rules. That's what we are going to cover in this section.

- We need a process to make the transition from a price-driven business plan to a value-and-experience-based business plan, and that's what we are going to cover in the next part of this book.

The 12 rules we need to follow to successfully transition to charging what we are worth

One of my goals with writing this book is to make sure I really spell out how to go about this very significant shift from being a poverty-based business to a really profitable business. Much of the move to becoming the most expensive – and enjoying the benefits that this brings – comes from our state of mind. In other words, we need to get our head right to make it work.

My 12 rules are based on my experience of moving to the 'most expensive' category and also helping many other businesses do the same. At the end of the day, it all came back to overcoming the inner demons and the limiting beliefs that were simply not true.

But having prosperous thoughts isn't enough, just as being positive about losing 20kg isn't enough without taking some serious action. So the rules we need to follow to start charging what we are truly worth need to be a combination of the two: changing your mindset *and* taking serious action.

Here are the 12 rules. We'll look at them individually in the following chapters.

RULE #1. You have to be absolutely, totally COMMITTED.

RULE #2. You have to REPROGRAMME your thinking.

RULE #3. You need to COMPARE yourself to your competitors by different markers, not just price.

RULE #4. You must create EXTRAORDINARY customer experiences.

RULE #5. You have to develop a TWO-WAY loyalty flow.

RULE #6. You must INVEST in this process.

RULE #7. You have to find a ROLE MODEL business.

RULE #8. Be very slow to DISCOUNT.

RULE #9. Use smart VALUE ADDING as the tool to grow sales.

RULE #10. Getting EVERY single sale should never be the goal.

RULE #11. Be crystal clear on which products and services you make MONEY on.

RULE #12. Do everything you can to stay RELEVANT to your customers.

I suggest printing these rules out and sticking them up somewhere where you'll easily see them (such as on the fridge or next to your computer screen), and checking in on them daily, especially when you start to get nervous (and you will) about making the leap from being cheap to being the most expensive.

RULE #1. You have to be absolutely, totally COMMITTED.

This transformation won't work unless you are absolutely, positively, one hundred percent committed to it. And in many instances, we need to 'burn the boats' to really make it work. You can't dabble at being the most expensive, or give it a bit of a go and then scurry back to the reassuring comfort of selling stuff because it's cheap.

We need to make the very conscious decision to become the best at what we do and to charge accordingly. If you can't make this commitment, there is little point in going forward because it just won't work, and that's why there are always only a few businesses at the top end of the price range and a huge number of businesses at the cheapest end of the range.

Think long and hard about how your current way of doing business has worked for you and how it has failed you. I know I became sick and tired of working my butt off for years with very little to show for it, and with very little prospect of that ever changing. I committed to charging more when I was finally over not charging enough.

Think about your future – how does it look? Think about the time and effort you put into doing what you do – surely you deserve to be paid a great price for what you deliver? Right here, right now, either commit fully or put this book down and forget about the idea of being the most expensive, because without a serious commitment it will never happen, and you'll probably just make your problems worse.

RULE #2. You have to REPROGRAMME your thinking.

A lot of our thinking around what we charge is based on what we think our customers can afford to pay. From my experience this thinking is incredibly flawed, for two reasons. Firstly, our customers *can* afford to pay more, but they won't with our current product or service offering because it's not worth more. And secondly, we are thinking only about our existing customers, who were generally drawn to us in the first place because of price. Simple solution: find new customers who are prepared to pay what you are charging when you increase your prices.

Many years back I had a travel business and our job was to sell tours to British tourists travelling to Cairns and the Great Barrier Reef. At the time I was young, I had some money behind me, and I sold how I would buy. For me, if I was travelling to Cairns for a big holiday, I would want to do just about everything – *everything* – that was on offer. Trips to the Great Barrier Reef, helicopter rides, balloon rides, nice meals, good wine – you get the idea. My average sale was about $1000 per person.

My sister worked for me at the time. She was a young mum, cash was tight, and everything in her world was budget driven. And that's exactly how she thought. She couldn't imagine spending $1000 over a few days while on holiday. Her average sale? It was $300 per person.

This is the best and most powerful illustration I have to show just how much impact our thinking has on what we charge and what we sell. Was I a better salesperson than my sister? Not at all. We both sold the same things: a trip out to the Great Barrier Reef, a day tour to a place called Kuranda on a train and skysail cable car, and a trip to the Daintree Rainforest. The difference was that I sold the top-of-the-line tours and she sold the bottom-of-the-line tours.

So with this rule, we need to identify where our poverty mentality is showing itself for us personally. How is it influencing the way we think and the decisions we are making every day?

To charge what we are worth – and even more significantly, to be the most expensive – we need to have a mindset that is full of abundance. And it's hard to think like this when you've spent a lot of your life struggling to pay your bills.

We have to start understanding and identifying our limiting beliefs around money and the thinking that's holding us back financially (and probably in many other ways). Generally this means we have to stop thinking about what we expect someone can afford and start charging what we are worth. The minute you start looking someone up and down asking yourself if they could afford you, you're already losing. I'm constantly surprised by the people who pay me the most, because they are rarely the ones I would expect to pay the most.

Start thinking more about value, about worth, about what you are bringing to the table, and what the customer is actually going to get. Check yourself as soon as you start having those negative, poverty-mentality-based thoughts we all know so well.

RULE #3. You need to COMPARE yourself to your competitors by different markers, not just price.

To say we are the cheapest, or have the best prices, feels like such a compelling sales pitch. But in my opinion, it's about the laziest sales pitch we can do. Really, there is no need for a salesperson: just put up a sign saying 'we are the cheapest'. Think back to what I spoke about earlier in this book. When all you can sell is the fact that you are the cheapest, you will only attract price-driven customers who have absolutely no loyalty to you, your business or your brand.

If you find yourself having sales conversations where your prices are being compared to your competitors, you need to come up with new and better options – or more specifically, far more compelling reasons for someone to buy from you other than your price.

The aim here is to showcase what makes you different to your competition, either in terms of specific products or services, or perhaps it's with credibility by showcasing the people or businesses you have worked with in the past, the milestones your business has achieved and the strategies you have for the future. Describe how you have developed what it is that you do; tell a better story around it.

The other interesting approach here is to ask better questions of your customers. Often a sales conversation ends up becoming a one-way stream of data about a product that often goes above the customer's head or their level of interest. The most engaging and most successful salespeople ask really smart questions, and they keep them coming. This not only shows they are interested in their customer and their needs but also allows them to talk about the features that are most important to the customer. Price is the last part of the conversation, and if you've done a great job, it's just a formality before the sale is concluded.

RULE #4. You must create EXTRAORDINARY customer experiences.

One of the backbone premises of this book and my entire principle of 'someone has to be the most expensive, why not make it you? But if you *are* going to be the most expensive, you also have to be the best' is that last part – you have to be the best.

I know I talk about this a lot in this book, and I do so unapologetically. You can't charge the most and deliver the least. It just doesn't work.

One of the ways we can really position ourselves as the best is with our customer experience. I've spoken about the shift in customer expectations – we are all moving from accepting transactions to demanding experiences. We are happy to buy from a business, but we want the experience to be memorable, wonderful, rewarding, rich – or whatever other descriptive word you want to slot in here.

This movement is happening around the world, and it will probably be the topic of my next book. I have a fascination with the concept of moving from transactions to experiences, and I've had the great pleasure of talking about it to packed auditoriums in countries as diverse as Iran and India.

I've come across so many examples of businesses in every corner of the planet really going above and beyond when it comes to creating extraordinary experiences for their customers, simply because they know how important it is.

Just one example I came across recently was an Italian outdoor clothing retailer who built a freezer room in their store to simulate below-zero conditions outdoors. Customers are encouraged to try on their potential purchases and spend time in the chiller to see just how warm their new clothing and outdoor adventure accessories will be. Did this experience increase sales? Absolutely. Did it generate a pile of free publicity? Absolutely.

So rule #4 needs you to be thinking about how you deliver your products and services, how you communicate, how you educate, your marketing, your instore customer experience through to your online customer experience – with the ultimate goal being to make it all as extraordinary as you can.

Remember, customers are generally won or lost over the little things, not the big things. Spend time looking for ways to do what others either won't do or can't do. You've got to find your own style of special sauce and deliver it constantly. This means having better conversations with your team, your customers, your advisors, your family, your friends – always be hungry to create a better experience for your customers.

RULE #5. You have to develop a TWO-WAY loyalty flow.

A little while back I heard an amazing story about a small business based in South Australia called Spring Gully. This family business was formed in 1946, by a Mr Edward McKee, who realised there was a market for his homemade pickled onions. Over the years, Spring Gully's product range diversified into all manner of pickles, jams, sauces, chutneys and spreads, and to this day it remains a family business.

Out of the blue, one Friday morning, Spring Gully sent out a very simple media release, stating that after all these years in business, they were being forced to close their doors. They were struggling to keep up in a world dominated by giant global manufacturers and the equally challenging retail food cartel that exists in Australia. Spring Gully's management were concerned that if they didn't shut the doors now, they might not be able to pay their staff all of their entitlements, something they couldn't live with.

While this simple media release went unnoticed by most, a small handful of people did indeed notice it and they were mortified to think that their favourite manufacturer of beautiful products which they had grown up with was simply going to close down with little more than a whimper. They leapt into action.

The 'Save Spring Gully' movement began. Radio stations jumped on board, followed closely by all media in South Australia and beyond. Soon it became national news, and there were even protests in the streets, with loyal customers holding their placards proudly, encouraging all South Australians to get behind this iconic local brand.

Having their customers fight for them like this was amazing, and humbling ... but would it be enough to save the company?

As media attention grew, and the shelves became bare of Spring Gully foods as people starting stockpiling their favourite condiments, a formerly unimagined white knight appeared. The first of the two largest food retailers in Australia put in a huge multi-million-dollar order to Spring Gully, which was enough to keep them going. The second of the big food retailers quickly followed, with another multi-million-dollar order, and Spring Gully was back in business, and it remains that way today.

Now, would these giant retailers have acted the way they did if Spring Gully's customers hadn't fought for them? I seriously doubt it. Regardless, they did, and it made me think long and hard, and ask myself a question: would my customers fight to save my business if I needed them to? And I think that's a question we all need to ask.

I think my customers would fight for my business. I don't say that with anything but humility and gratitude, because I know the people who buy my products and services. I treat them with absolute respect. I value them. I support them. And I will always go above and beyond the call of duty for them. This is a conscious decision.

My question to you that forms the backbone of this rule: how do *you* show loyalty to *your* customers? If you don't give loyalty, how can you possibly expect to receive it? Of course, the underlying issue when we sell based on little other than price is that we attract those customers who will never be loyal to a business, because they are always looking for the cheapest price and they move their business around accordingly.

We all need to look for ways to not just tell our customers that they mean a great deal to us, but to also show them. We need to be prepared to support the people who buy from us, however we can, whenever we can. Do this and, when you need them the most, you might be surprised by just how hard they will fight for you.

RULE #6. You must INVEST in this process.

Whenever I'm working with a client helping them to make the transition of moving from the cheapest to the most expensive, or as a minimum putting up their rates so they actually start to make some money, I warn them that they are going to have to invest in this process.

They are going to have to invest time, because they will need to change a lot of things, such as their website copy and design, promotional material, possibly their branding, their office furnishings, their uniform and their packaging. Now, I don't say you should change all of this overnight, but more often than not, considerable changes will be needed to reposition your business. This means you have to be prepared to invest in the process.

Earlier on I shared the story about buying a new car and the lack of service that led me to buying a car worth twice as much as I had intended to pay when I finally received some good service. The car I bought was a brand new Audi A6, and it was a very nice car. I have to say, I felt more successful when I got in my new car. I started to dress better when I drove it. I was proud to park it in the car park where my business was located. I was proud to park outside my clients' offices instead of around the corner (anyone done that before?).

Not long after this purchase, I had a meeting with a new client. This company was a property developer and the owner was very wealthy and clearly very successful on many levels. As I left the meeting, he walked me out to my car so we could chat and finalise a few details. When I got to my car he complimented me on it, saying what a beautiful car it was. He then said: 'When I engage a consultant, I want the best consultant I can find. I want the one driving the expensive car, and all that this entails, not the one driving the old bomb. If you look successful I'm halfway to believing that you are good at what you do. What other people say about you tells me the rest of what I need to know.'

Now, I get that some of you might be reading this and saying, 'how shallow', or, 'an expensive car is no measure of someone's ability'. I agree with you. But, and this is a big but, how this expensive car makes you feel and the message it sends to your existing and prospective clients says a lot about you. Check whether your poverty mentality is being triggered here.

I'm not saying you have to go out and buy a Maserati as part of this transformation, but I do think you need to look the part, and feel the part. If you're going to be the most expensive and by association be the best, let it show.

OK, buy the Maserati ...

RULE #7. You have to find a ROLE MODEL business.

Find your role model business (it doesn't have to be in the same industry as you). Find that business that just seems to get it right. That business which has that certain confidence and ability to constantly deliver on their promise, that other people talk about and recommend and that is, without a doubt, the most expensive.

Learn from this business. Study everything they do. Buy their products or services if you can. Ask people about them. Sit outside the business if it's a bricks-and-mortar-type business and see what kind of people come and go. Look at their marketing, their social media, their website, their promotional material. Talk to their staff. Find out as much as you can about the things that make this business tick. Even interview the owner of the business if you can. How did they develop this culture, and why? Learn, learn, learn.

Once you've learned everything you can from this business, find another one. And then learn everything you can about 'being the best' from this business.

Become a student of these businesses' strategies and you will naturally gravitate towards them in your own business.

RULE #8. Be very slow to DISCOUNT.

I'm surprised at how often salespeople offer me a discount before I've even asked for one. I simply fail to understand why. In most instances I was never going to ask for a discount; why would I? Yet the salesperson is doing their thing and then, out of the blue, they tell me that they can do it for a better price. All I've done is sit there and nod my head.

Once again, this to me shows a lack of confidence in the product or service. And many businesses throw away a huge amount of money (which means profit, cash that could have been in the business owner's bank account) simply by being too quick to discount.

We live in a world where people will generally ask for a discount if it's on their mind. Let's address that in a second. But why on earth would you offer a discount before there is even a mention of it? The answer is generally 'I could tell that the customer was price driven'. My question to that is, how? By what they were wearing, by their body language, by some innate sixth sales sense? No, it's because we think we will get the sale if we lower the price, and it's a typical sign of a poverty mentality and a lazy approach to selling.

One of the best things I did in my business was stop discounting when people asked me to. My standard line was: 'We aren't in Bali – haggling over price is not a part of our culture or my business. I focus on absolutely, positively over-delivering on your expectations, and that's what I'll do, as opposed to being resentful to you because I felt obligated to lower the price.' The more I adopted this stance, the more people stopped asking. I respected myself enough to stop discounting; they picked up on that and started to look for quality, not lower prices.

Now, don't get me wrong, there are times that I will do a special offer of some sort in my coaching business. I do this strategically, when I have extra capacity, as a way to develop new clients. But I do it on my terms, when it suits me, when it fits my overall plan and strategy, and I do it in very limited quantities.

If you automatically go to offer a discount, odds are your staff will as well. Over time, this has probably become a comfortable habit to close the deal. It needs to be broken. Ask better questions. When there is that awkward moment of tension and you've finished telling a customer about a product or service, ask them what they think as opposed to awkwardly offering them a discount. It will be uncomfortable at first; it always is when it comes to changing ingrained behaviour, but the first time you do it, and the customer still buys, and you realise you haven't given away a pile of money for no reason, you will like that feeling. And you will do it again and again and again.

In the next part of this book I'm going to be talking about the process we need to take to become the business that is the most expensive, and I'll be talking about the language we use and the stories we tell. You'll get a good understanding for what I mean by having better conversations around money with ourselves and with our customers.

RULE #9. Use smart VALUE ADDING as the tool to grow sales.

Now, having spoken about discounting and agreed that automatic, non-strategic, lazy selling by offering discounts upfront is a thing of the past, it's time to talk about value adding. Read any business book and someone is going to say value add over discounting every day of the week, and I agree.

But for some people, even though they value add, it really is just a sheep dressed in a wolf's clothing. By this I mean it's really just another form of discounting, without any clear plan or strategy. Value adding as a strategic tool is smart and, if done well, will be far more effective than just giving stuff away (like giving money away).

Let me give you an example. As a professional speaker, I charge a significant amount to deliver a presentation to an audience. Often I get asked to discount, especially if I'm being asked to deliver more than one presentation. But instead of using that nasty 'D word', I look for strategic ways to add value. I might ask the company booking me if their team could benefit from a sales training workshop at the conference as a value add, or perhaps if they are having an awards night, I might offer to MC the event for free as a value add.

Now, both of these value adds have a purpose: they introduce the client to two new product offerings of mine – sales training and MC'ing – that they previously haven't used. I get to showcase a new skillset and they get an added service which has considerable perceived value (and a high value in reality). We both win. I have to do some extra work, but not a great deal in reality.

My advice is to look for ways to value add that let you showcase other products and services your client could ultimately start to buy somewhere down the line. Think more creatively, and certainly more strategically, when it comes to how you value add.

I was buying some goat cheese from a local market the other day – this cheese is amazing. It certainly is expensive, and it certainly is some of the best goat cheese I've ever tasted. A few weeks back when I went to buy my normal cheese, they were offering a new type of cheese at half price with every sale. So I bought one, and it is sensational. Now when I go to the market, I buy one of each kind. This means this producer has increased my weekly purchases by one hundred percent. Imagine the impact it would have on their yearly bottom line if one hundred customers a week doubled their purchase.

Anyway, you get the point. Value add smartly, wisely and strategically. Use it to introduce new products and services, without eroding the revenue you are making from your main product.

RULE #10. Getting EVERY single sale should never be the goal.

I often encounter business owners who proudly say they get every job they quote on, as if this is a mark of how good their business is. To me it says they are grossly under-charging for what they do, and it is certainly not something to be proud of.

I work on the principle that if I'm getting about fifty percent of the jobs I quote on, my pricing is about right. If I get them all, I'm way too cheap, and if I get none of them, I'm probably way too expensive (or I've got the wrong customers I'm trying to sell my products and services to).

Our goal should never be to get *every* job, even when we change our pricing and become the most expensive – in fact, it's clearly the exact opposite. We should aim to be working with people who respect what we do, who are willing to pay for quality and who pay promptly – that is certainly not everyone.

This shift in thinking can often take a while to settle in. As I mentioned way back at the start of this book, the biggest shift that needs to take place is to move from a poverty mentality in business to a prosperity mentality. Some of the ideas I suggest will certainly make you feel uncomfortable, and as I said, this shift is not for the faint of heart. But if you can make the shift in thinking, the rewards are astonishing.

RULE # 11. Be crystal clear on which products and services you make MONEY on.

One thing that many businesses, if not most businesses, are guilty of is not actually knowing which products and services make them money. We automatically assume the higher the product pricing the more profit that is made. Surprisingly, this is not always the case.

I always remember a website developer friend of mine say that if they are really honest with themselves, they make more money out of selling a simple, one-page website for $599 than they do on larger website projects, sometimes worth over $20,000. This may seem hard to understand, but it's not when you break it down.

The one-page sites are templated and are basically automatic to set up; they require a few minutes from a developer to ensure everything is working and that the site is not illegal in any way. So, pretty much all of the $599 is profit. Let's be generous and say the cost is $99, so each one-page site makes a profit of $500. If they could sell ten of these a day they could retire happy and one person could run the business.

With larger projects there is clearly a lot more work, more team members involved, more room for error, bigger expectations from clients and a whole lot more that can go wrong. Some projects work well and they make good money from them, others are disasters and they can end up losing money. It can be hit and miss, and smart, proactive and timely project management is the key to making this side of the business work.

Now, clearly from a business point of view, it would seem to make more sense to focus all their energy on selling and building as many one-page sites as they possibly can, simply because they never, ever lose money on them. And as the old saying goes: 'I've never heard of a business going broke because it was making a profit'. So why do these developers do the other bigger and more risky projects?

The answer is interesting. They do them because they are stimulating, the team thrives on the challenge, there is a much bigger sense of satisfaction from building websites for larger clients, and when they do make money, they make good money.

Often the reason for offering a particular product or service extends beyond just making money from it. But what I like about this successful company's approach is that they know their numbers, they know which projects are profitable and which ones are not. Do you know the same for your products and services?

It's all well and good to charge more for what we sell, and even to be the most expensive, but do it with a clear understanding of what you currently make money on and what you are currently losing money on. This means being really honest with ourselves, and taking the time to work out the exact costs as well as the amount of time we spend on a specific product or service. We need information, and we need it to be accurate.

When I work with clients to figure out where they currently make money or lose money, they are virtually always surprised and, more often than not, shocked. The things they think they make money on often aren't profitable, and that is hard to get your head around.

Having worked with some really smart people in the restaurant game, the depth of analysis they put into menu engineering – which is not just working out the right kinds of food to serve, but working out the actual cost per plate of food, the cost per cup of coffee, per drink, per serve of garlic bread – is amazing. Experts in this space can look at a menu and tell you straightaway if the restaurant has any chance of making money – regardless of how busy it may be. They can scan through a menu and see the unprofitable items straightaway based on the time required to make the dish, the equipment required, the ingredients required and the cost.

Another common issue I come across is ridiculously simple mathematical mistakes that are catastrophic to the business. One example comes to mind.

I was contacted by a lady who ran a series of very specialised magazines that were sold on subscription. Her business was based in Australia, but most of her subscribers were based in the US and Canada. The magazines she produced were high quality, in the craft space, containing lots of patterns and practical advice. When I visited her office it was filled with lots of lovely grannies all making stuff.

Anyway, she contacted me for some help because a few months back they had run their biggest ever campaign in the US and it was hugely successful, but something was wrong and they had run out of money with six months left of magazines to supply and they simply couldn't put their finger on what the issue was. And this is common as well; we get too close to the problem and we don't think to ask the obvious questions.

I went down the obvious path – were they collecting the money? Yes, everyone who had subscribed had paid upfront, and there were about 10,000 people. So they had started with a huge chunk of money in the bank to cover the 12 months of producing and distributing the magazine, which had basically disappeared halfway through.

The owner was worried about theft, increased operational costs, higher production costs, bank fees – all kinds of things. What made it all a little more awkward was that her husband was the financial controller and even he couldn't put his finger on what the issue was.

I quickly realised there was a problem with the numbers, but the problem wasn't any of the other things that they suspected, it was the maths used to work out the cost of the offer they had used in the campaign. They were offering six magazines, including postage, over a 12-month period. I looked at all the costs, and it was soon clear that the costs were worked out for four magazines in a year not six – so basically they were losing about US$50 per subscription, and that meant their most successful campaign ever was going to cost them $500,000, which they didn't have. A simple mathematical error ended this business.

The bottom line: know what products and services you are making money on, and know which ones you are losing money on. And from now on, make a point of always knowing this information no matter how much you charge for anything.

RULE #12. Do everything you can to stay RELEVANT to your customers.

You might not be aware of it, but every single business, including yours and mine, is in a battle to stay relevant with our customers. And this is a battle that once lost, the war is over.

So, what do I really mean here?

As we've discussed earlier in the book, modern consumers have so much choice it's almost unbelievable. Add to this their love of everything new and consumers' appetites for trying and expecting new, new, new, our job as business owners is to keep up. This means we have to stay relevant to our customers, because if we lose relevance, it's unlikely we will ever get it back.

Relevance can be lost because a business fails to keep up with the changing needs and expectations of customers. Think Blockbuster – a prime example. A global chain and a business worth hundreds of millions of dollars that saw the streaming revolution coming, but instead of them becoming Netflix before Netflix, they did nothing and slowly went broke. I spoke to a man a little while back who had owned seven Blockbuster franchises in Western Australia. He said everyone at the company knew the writing was on the wall if they didn't change and change rapidly, but somehow they just watched the disaster unfold and did nothing. Sadly they lost relevance and faded away.

And this is a big point. Blockbuster didn't do anything wrong by their customers. In fact, for most of us a journey to Blockbuster to get a pile of videos and then DVDs on a Friday night was a mandatory part of the week. We loved it. We would all wait and pounce on someone returning a latest release movie.

So there was no issue with Blockbuster's offering, they just lost relevance as the more logical and more cost-effective world of 'streaming' evolved as new technology developed. And of course, now with all the different streaming companies, about 15 in total, they are all fighting to figure out their relevance. I've got no doubt that streaming will look different in a few years. It will evolve and morph once again, based on who has the most logical and appealing offer.

Staying relevant to our customers means staying connected to our customers. We need to communicate directly with them all the time. We need to be aware of the trends, the changes, the challenges, the opportunities. We need to look at new companies starting up. What is changing? How do we stay connected and how do we stay relevant?

Business has become much more dynamic these days. There is no set-and-forget mode, which in many ways was the business model of the past. We have to constantly be evolving, fine-tuning, trying new things, getting some of them wrong, and telling bigger and better stories about what we do and why we do it.

The battle for relevance is here, and it's here to stay. Remember, once you lose relevance you will never get it back.

★ ★ ★

These rules keep us on the right path. They are the important considerations and strategies that we need to work on daily. They will help our transition to becoming the most expensive and enjoying the benefits this brings to our business and our life if we follow them rigorously, no matter how hard that might prove to be, particularly in the early stages of your shift.

Part IX

THE PROCESS WE NEED TO FOLLOW

You can't just put lipstick on a wombat...

Where are you now on your road to becoming the most expensive?

PART I: The BIG why ...

PART II: The world has changed – have you?

PART III: There are many very good reasons to be the most expensive

PART IV: How scared does this idea make you?

PART V: So what does it actually mean to be the best?

PART VI: Does this concept really work for any kind of business in any market?

PART VII: Surely the online world is completely different? Or is it?

PART VIII: Now we are convinced of the reasoning, we need some rules to work with

PART IX: The process we need to follow

PART X: Now it's time to rethink what we say

PART XI: More ways to increase your credibility, trustworthiness and 'buyability'

Part XII: This road is not for the faint of heart

WE'VE SPENT A LOT OF TIME getting ready; now it's time to walk through the steps you need to take to make this transition to being the most expensive, or at least starting to charge what you are worth.

I have a simple, 10-step process. Each step is equally important, and they need to be followed and implemented in order. As I've mentioned often, you can't half do this – you are either in or you are out. Each of these steps plays a major role in the transformation of moving from a price-driven, undercharging business to a business that charges what it is worth.

Here are the steps to make this happen:

STEP #1. Create a bigger, better and more compelling VISION OF YOUR FUTURE.

STEP #2. Develop your PLAN to make the transformation.

STEP #3. Get everyone who needs to be ONBOARD, onboard.

STEP #4. Define how you are going to BE THE BEST.

STEP #5. You can't put lipstick on a wombat. Do something BIG AND BOLD.

STEP #6. Tell a new, bigger, bolder STORY. Be raw, real and authentic.

STEP #7. Get more CREATIVE with your pricing.

STEP #8. Create EXTRAORDINARY EXPERIENCES for your customers.

STEP #9. Be prepared to let everything old go. Make room for everything NEW.

STEP #10. Stay on the PATH.

To really show how we can apply this process, I'm going to use an experience of mine as an example to guide you through the steps. It came when I was running a simple marketing company, providing good advice to clients who couldn't afford to pay. Most of my clients were small businesses, fairly marginal in many instances. I was working ridiculously long hours, charging about a third of what I should have been charging, and was totally locked into the belief that I could never change.

Sadly, I'd forgotten most of my experiences with my first business, my dive shop, where I had battled these demons all those years ago and won. But as life often does, when we don't really learn our lessons, we end up back in the same situation.

STEP #1. Create a bigger, better and more compelling VISION OF YOUR FUTURE.

Way back at the beginning of this book I wrote about the need to be really clear on our big WHY. And at the same time, if we don't have a bigger, better, more compelling vision of our future, we will never have the courage and the determination to make the changes I'm suggesting. In fact, the same applies for making any significant change in our life. Unless we have a big enough reason to change, an incredibly compelling outcome to look forward to and to keep us on track, change rarely lasts. We might start strong, but over time, we slide back into our old habits. It's what we humans do.

For me, creating a bigger, better and more compelling vision for my future came down to a number of things. Firstly, I was slowly killing myself. I was working really hard, I was overweight (and I mean overweight as in 50kg overweight at least), I wasn't exercising, I was working seven days a week for at least 14 hours a day, often more. I was struggling financially. I was busy all the time but never really making any money. I was a heart attack waiting to happen. And I wasn't very happy about life.

It was about this time I got a phone call that changed my life. It was my brother-in-law ringing to tell me my sister had just dropped dead of a heart attack. I was of course stunned, incredibly upset and totally heartbroken. Wendy and I were orphans, we had been together all of our lives, and had shared many very hard experiences growing up. My greatest fear in life was losing her — and it had happened.

Slowly over the coming months, my grief started to lessen and I began to take stock of my own life. I realised things needed to change or it would be me dropping dead next. Two areas of my life needed urgent attention: my health and my business. I realised that the two were tied together in some strange way: my business had always been my number one priority in life, it was something I could control, I could be proud of and I could rely upon. But what use is a successful business if you're dead?

I started to get very clear about how I wanted my life to look, how I wanted to feel, and even how I wanted to look. I certainly became clear about how I wanted my business to be. I was tired of the struggle, tired of everything feeling so hard all the time. I know many of you reading this will understand how this feels. Year after year, battling a sense of being stuck in the same place, no matter how hard you try to move forward.

I was writing copious pages of notes, about the things I didn't want in my life anymore as much as the things I did want. I was getting clearer on how I wanted my life to look on a daily basis. What did I have to stop? What did I have to start? My clarity grew. I knew I now had a very compelling vision of my future. I didn't know how I was going to achieve it, but at this stage I didn't need to know. I simply believed that where I was heading was better than where I was now. And I had no doubt that this was the way to get out of any bad situation: start with a compelling, clear vision of a future that is far better than your present.

STEP #2. Develop your PLAN to make the transformation.

So I set about formulating a plan to completely change my world. It was a big plan, a bold plan, and it wasn't going to be easy. That said, the alternative was much worse. I knew my plan had two elements: lose weight and get healthy, and completely change my business.

The first was probably the easiest in many ways. I was smart enough to know what I needed to do to lose weight – move more, eat less. But I had to build time into my world to exercise, to de-stress, to eat better, to simply take better care of myself. So I developed a plan that detailed what I thought I needed to do.

Then it was time to focus on my business. I knew I needed to make dramatic changes, and I realised I was in exactly the same place that I was with my dive shop all those years ago. My current business was failing for all the same reasons that my dive shop was failing when I first bought it:

1. I wasn't charging enough for my services, to the point that no matter how busy I was I could never get ahead.

2. I had the wrong kinds of customers, who really were totally price-driven. They didn't value my knowledge and advice, and it showed.

3. I had all the limiting beliefs imaginable: 'the market is too tight', 'people can't afford to pay more', 'I'm not good enough', and on and on it went.

4. I was exactly the same as every other marketing company in town. I hadn't done anything to differentiate myself.

So, what did I do to turn my dive shop around? It became very clear that I now needed to do exactly the same things, do the things that I know work and transform my business. And that was the moment I realised that someone has to be the most expensive marketing company in town, why not make it me? But to be the most expensive I needed to be the best. I set about developing my plan to make this happen.

Here's what I included in my business plan:

• I was very specific about my compelling future.

• I was clear about how much I wanted to charge and how much I wanted to make.

• I knew what kind of clients I wanted (ones that could afford me, and who would respect me and the advice I offered and the work I did).

• I knew I had to make some dramatic physical changes, move office, change the business name, rebrand completely. I would treat this as a new business.

- I had to make sure I could afford to make these changes, because I knew I'd lose some customers initially – business would get worse before it got better.

- And I'd need some help.

Like all successful ventures, the better we plan the more likely they are to succeed. Give your new business every opportunity to win – plan well.

STEP #3. Get everyone who needs to be ONBOARD, onboard.

Making dramatic changes, regardless of whether they are personal changes or business changes, generally requires help from others. Who do we need to enlist to make the necessary changes?

From a health point of view, I set about a serious weight loss regime. I enlisted an incredible personal trainer, Kelly Sinclair, who has become one of my dearest friends. Through many intense afternoons of sweat and toil, combined with yoga and better eating choices, I managed to lose a big chunk of the extra weight and get much healthier. It's something I still battle with to this day, but I'm in much better shape now than I was back then. (I'll leave the health side of things out of the process as we move forward from here. I want to focus on helping you to start charging what you are worth. But I will say, when you do this, it's surprising what else changes in your life. It's all about self-worth more than net worth.)

Back to my marketing company. I needed to enlist the aid of the team, my staff and my suppliers. I had to make sure I had the plan clear in my own head before selling it to everyone else, knowing full well to expect some pushback, which I did receive.

I also knew that to make this transformation effective and successful I would need everyone on board, and from my experience in the past, it was unlikely that everyone would be able to make the move from being a price-driven business to a high-quality, 'be the most expensive' business. And of course, I was right. There were casualties along the way, people who needed to move on, and this created the opportunity for them to do exactly that.

For the most part, my little team was excited but nervous about this ambitious move. We had been the little marketing company hidden away behind a ridiculously long name – Australian Business and Marketing Solutions (try getting the domain name for that) or the acronym ABMS, which means as much as ZRFS. We spoke a lot, we discussed the plan, we got strategic, and we got ready to make our move.

I started to notice a shift. The more we spoke about this 'new business', and the more we discussed and planned what it would look like, the less nervous we became and the more excited we started to get.

I've noticed this when working with other businesses. The initial discussions and ideas are tough. People get uncomfortable – all their fears, limiting beliefs and stories that they tell themselves start to come up. And that in turn tends to create pushback. There are all kinds of fear-based questions. Most of them can be eliminated by answering the most important question for the team members: 'What impact will this have on me?' Address this and you are on your way to a much smoother transition.

STEP #4. Define how you are going to BE THE BEST.

I spoke a great deal about what it means to be the best earlier in the book. There is a lot that can define what this means to not only us, but also to our customers. The most important point I'd like to reiterate is that being the best is rarely something that happens accidentally. It's a conscious decision, a very strategic plan and a goal – and the best way to achieve any goal is to be very specific about it.

I'm sure you've read plenty of stuff about setting goals, the need to write them down, read them often, put deadlines on them, make sure everyone on the team knows and understands the goal and how it's going to be achieved – all of that good, meaty goal-setting stuff. And it's all true. So the same applies for us to become the absolute best at what we do.

We need to:

1. Spell it out very clearly – for our use – exactly what being the best means to us.

2. Get strategic on how you're going to achieve this.

3. Make sure that everyone involved in your business (and your life) knows the plan.

4. Establish some clear-cut rules and boundaries.

5. Check in and review your progress every single day.

Now if I was to identify the areas you could be the best in, I'd break them into the following categories.

BE THE BEST WITH – the products and services that you sell

This is pretty obvious, right? Make great stuff. Not good stuff – *great* stuff. Offer great knowledge. Make whatever you are selling the absolute best that it can be and the best available in your market where possible. The only way to really do this is to know your competitors thoroughly – and I mean thoroughly. You have to be able to know, hand on heart, that what you sell really is the best in the marketplace where you operate, and this takes a high degree of humility, reality and research.

BE THE BEST WITH – the service you offer

There is always so much discussion around the concept of service, but let me be blunt – when was the last time you were absolutely blown away by the service you received? More often than not we are left completely underwhelmed. Ironically, sensational customer service will make up for products and services that are lacking every time. Being the best when it comes to the service you offer your customers is not that hard, yet it seems to be a lost art. Master this and you're well and truly on the path to being able to charge more.

Service tends to relate to speed, ease of purchase, delivering when promised, politeness and friendliness – how we as the customer feel in any transaction.

BE THE BEST WITH – your communication

This is a doozy. Communication remains one of the top reasons that customers are left unsatisfied with a buying experience. We all know what the line 'I'll get right back to you' generally means? We will never hear from that person again. I was speaking at an event for a pile of mortgage brokers a while back and I decided to do my own research to find out what people's biggest disappointment was when it came to using a mortgage broker. I did an informal survey on my social media, and got 400 responses. The most overwhelming response was that they always had to chase their mortgage broker. They never called when they said they were going to call. Ninety percent of the people who responded to my survey had the same issue. Now that is amazing.

The reality is that I think most mortgage brokers offer a similar service. If I was a mortgage broker and my aim was to be the best, I'd become the world's best communicator. I'd be on that phone ringing everyone back way before they expected it, just to show my customers that I was on top of everything.

I made this point in the opening of my presentation, and a man put up his hand and said, 'But sometimes we haven't got any news, we haven't heard back from the lender, so we've got nothing to say'. My response – you ring the client as promised and tell them you haven't got any news but you're all across it. This gives the client absolute confidence that you are on to it.

BE THE BEST WITH – staying relevant

The concept of staying relevant is really interesting to me, and is one that we are not discussing in business anywhere near enough in my opinion. It's becoming increasingly difficult to keep up with the expectations and needs of our customers, because they are changing so fast. We need to be incredibly proactive at staying relevant, and this is – once again – something we need to take conscious steps towards, every single day.

Some time back I was looking after the marketing of a large publicly listed construction company that was growing at an incredible rate. My little Cairns-based marketing company was fighting way above its weight, and we knew our risk was the company outgrowing us. This means we needed to look like we could manage their needs with ease. To me, this meant I had to think long and hard about what a capital city marketing agency would offer that would make them more appealing than my firm.

This got back to things like the size of the team, the expertise, use of technology, currency with marketing ideas, creativity and manpower. I invested a lot of time and money to make certain that we were across all these potential issues with training, equipment, attending conferences, employing great people – and going to great lengths to let our client know what we were doing.

To me, the key to staying relevant is staying connected with our customers. And this doesn't mean one-sided bombardment with emails and social media campaigns, it means engagement – a two-way flow of information and data.

Just about every product or service that I sell, including this book, has come about as a result of engagement with my customers. They tell me what their issues are, what their challenges are, what their needs are. And I listen. Intently.

If you make a point of asking the right questions, engaging and interacting with your customers, they will tell you what they want. And if you're smart, you will give it to them. I do retreats and programmes all over the world, on everything from writing books to becoming a professional speaker, and every one of these has come from people telling me that this is what they wanted.

I encounter so many businesses that simply lose relevance with their customers because they either don't know how to engage them or they don't like what they hear and they ignore what their customers are saying.

Recently I was engaged by the European Union to travel to England and run a series of 15 workshops around the country, helping businesses of all sizes to get ready for Brexit. They needed to work out how to brand and market themselves for international sales.

In every workshop I asked two questions to get the day started. Why should anyone buy what you are selling? And who do you want to sell it to? The responses were mind-boggling.

The overwhelming response to question one was: 'People should buy what we are selling because we are British.' And the overwhelming response to question two was: 'We want to sell into Europe.' So their entire international sales strategy was to try to sell their products and services to the countries they had just told to bugger off as part of Brexit, and their only key selling point was that they were British – at a time when being British was the least impressive sales feature imaginable. When I questioned these business owners about their thinking, I was met with blank stares. Scary stuff indeed.

Anyway, you get the point I'm sure. We need to stay relevant with our customers as a survival strategy, but really smart businesses actually come up with a product or service almost before we know we need it, and we can't wait to buy it. This doesn't happen by accident or genius, it happens with engagement and an attitude of respect for our customers.

★ ★ ★

So, we have four areas where we can really position ourselves as being the best, and charge accordingly. If you really want to be the most expensive, and by association be the absolute best at what you do, aim to tick the box for all four. And this is going to require some deep thinking, a high level of commitment, and daily discussion about each of these four areas.

STEP #5. You can't put lipstick on a wombat. Do something BIG AND BOLD.

OK, this is the backbone of the transformation. You can't just triple your rates and make no other changes. You will lose your customers, and end up with a business that no one wants to buy from. Small cosmetic changes are unlikely to work in the short term, and I'm assuming you're keen to adopt this new model relatively quickly.

When I had my dive shop I made radical changes. I changed the name, the branding to go with the name, the internal look and feel of the shop, the equipment we sold, our marketing – everything down to what our instructors wore. For all intents and purposes we became a new business, with how the business looked and our attitude.

The point is, we need to draw a line in the sand between the business we were and the business we are becoming. This line needs to be very clear and very well defined. I had to approach my marketing business the same way.

The first thing I decided was that we needed to move our office. And if we were going to move, we needed to move to be among the types of businesses we wanted as clients. There was one high-rise building that was considered the corporate heart of town and that would have been perfect.

Now, with my old poverty mentality I would never, ever have thought about moving into that office building. The rent was known to be the most expensive in town. As those words popped into my head, and made me stop and think, I realised that if the rent is the most expensive in that building, and it attracted the most successful businesses in town, my business needed to be there.

So I headed down to speak to the lady who handled the leasing for the building, expecting it to be way out of my budget. And it was, but I rented an office on the ground floor and ended up having that office for almost 12 years. It was big, they fitted it out for me and made it look amazing. Now I had a big flash office in a big flash building in the most expensive part of town, with lots of potential clients, hopefully all in need of the best marketing company in town. Next we needed a new name. Something simple, strong and confident. We rebranded to 'The Marketing Professionals'. The name said it all. I got a new logo and company brand developed by a friend of mine who was the best graphic designer in town at the time. Slowly the plan was coming together.

Now, I know that what I've done (twice) has been big and bold. But as the title of this step states, you can't put lipstick on a wombat, meaning you can't just tart things up a little and expect everyone to not recognise that it's the same old business trying to charge a pile more.

What do you need to do that is big and bold? One of the biggest and easiest steps is to change your business name. It's effective, it wipes the slate clean, and it lets you rewrite the rules. I often get people freaking out when I suggest this. 'What if we lose all of our customers with a name change?' they ask. Great – you need new customers anyway, otherwise we would not be having this conversation.

Business owners get overly attached to their company names. I've done hundreds of rebrands for businesses, where we've completely changed the company name and the branding and never had any negative issues. And more importantly, we live in a world that not only gets the need for reinvention, but welcomes reinvention. It all comes back to good planning and great communication. Get these two parts right and your customers will come along with you for the ride. Of course, whether you still want them or not will be determined by your new offer and pricing.

You need to decide what your big and bold thing is going to be. Is it to move office? Is it to get an office? Is it to rebrand completely? Is it to get rid of your office and move to being virtual? Is it to move to a new city? Is it to take on a new range of products and services under this new brand? Whatever doing something big and bold looks like for you, don't half do it. Remember, you can't just put lipstick on a wombat.

STEP #6. Tell a new, bigger, bolder STORY. Be raw, real and authentic.

The next part of this book is where we will be doing a deep dive on communication. It's all well and good to change our product and service offering, to aspire to be the best and really commit to that, to create amazing experiences for our customers and everything else I'm suggesting here, but we also need to tell bigger, bolder and more authentic stories to really connect with our customers.

Consumers are much more informed and educated these days. Do we really need to know that an accountant does tax? Or that a lawyer does law? Or that a mortgage broker gets us a mortgage? Yet we go out of our way to state the obvious – to me this is close to the top of the list of everyday marketing mistakes that are still ridiculously common. The mistake that is actually at the top of the list is the one where we go to great lengths to tell prospective customers how we are exactly the same as our competitors (go to two or three sites for any professional service businesses, hotel or airline and see how they basically all start by saying they are different and then go on to explain how they are exactly the same as their competitors).

We need to treat people with respect, and this starts by understanding that they know what we do. What they *don't* know is how we are different, why we started the business, our philosophy towards everything in business, the role we play in the community, our commitment to them, and so on. We can explain all of this in corporate gobbledygook – or we can simply tell better, more meaningful stories.

Tell the story of your business, warts and all. We love a good story that has lots of struggle and twists and turns, but where you ultimately win in the end. Tell stories about your people, your customers, your products, your history. Tell stories. Then tell more stories. And tell them everywhere. But more of this in the next section of this book when we dive deep on telling a new story about the new business you have become.

STEP #7. Get more CREATIVE with your pricing.

This step is always interesting. Business owners often don't think about *how* they price as opposed to the actual price. And right now, there are lots of changes to pricing structure and formats happening around the world.

Let's take a look at the subscription price model. Every month when you get your credit card bill, how many items are on there that are regular subscription-type items? Your phone plan, your internet, your streaming options, your music options, perhaps a newspaper subscription, various health and wellbeing apps, your gym membership? The list goes on, and it's getting longer every year. We are in the midst of a 'happy to pay a little every month as opposed to a lot in one hit' stage.

It's interesting to see that Burger King in the US just introduced a subscription model where customers pay a monthly fee and get all the coffee they want included in the deal. Burger King are no dummies; they've done their homework and realised that a subscription-based pricing model is good for business. How many people come in to get their subscription coffee and don't buy anything else? Not many I'm guessing.

In the book *Subscribed*, by Tien Tzuo, the author argues that the subscription model can and should be applied to everything from getting our monthly razor blades to buying a house. This is a great book to read if you want to dive a little deeper into the subscription pricing model. While I'm talking about smart books to challenge our thinking I would also strongly recommend the book *The Forever Transaction* by Robbie Baxter. This book is all about 'creating a subscription model so compelling your customers will never want to leave'.

In my business I sell a number of membership products, with a subscription pricing model, targeting specific niches. Whenever I present, I get a spike in sales, and with each membership sold being about $2000 a year, that's a lot of extra revenue.

The key here is to think a little differently about how you charge (not just *what* you charge). What can you do to make your pricing more appealing to your customers? And how can you actually charge more by being more creative?

I recently came across a company in the US that offers luxury cars available on a monthly payment plan. Now, I know there is nothing new with this idea, it's just a lease or a loan, but with this company, they do something very cool: you pay a monthly fee and you can swap the car you have. So you might like a Mercedes for a few months, then swap for an Audi, then a BMW, and so on. Ultimately you pay more for the flexibility and the ability to swap cars, but that's what makes their product offering different.

Think about professional services. How can you bundle up your pricing in a smarter way? A more appealing way? A more flexible way? Talk to your customers – that's a great place to start. Bottom line – get creative.

STEP #8. Create EXTRAORDINARY EXPERIENCES for your customers.

I've already gone to great lengths to talk about the need to move from *doing transactions* to *creating experiences*. Hopefully I've emphasised enough just how important this is and the opportunity that it represents. If I could do anything, it would be to spend all day, every day working with smart companies that have a desire to create extraordinary experiences.

If you want to increase what you charge, you need to get really smart and really creative at building experiences for your customers. It's as simple as that. Now, I know for many of us our products or services *are* the experience. If you are an incredible cheese maker, and one taste gets people hooked, that's a great experience. But there are so many more opportunities to enhance every customer's experience – I could quite literally rattle off hundreds of them.

So, where do we start? I tend to recommend doing something simple; it's called a touchpoint map or a customer experience map (or any variation of this kind of language). You simply map out every single touchpoint that your customers can have with your business, ideally in a chronological order. It might start at checking you out online or on social media, through to visiting your business, getting the product or service, using it, paying, leaving and then reflecting.

Once we have a touchpoint map, identify the high-value touch-points versus the low-value touchpoints and everything in between. Think about a visit to the dentist. Low-value touchpoints might be lighting in reception when you walk in, meaning it's not very important to the overall experience, whereas a high-value touch-point is the appearance (and smell) of the dentist. A cold, unfriendly, gruff, smelly dentist is not what we want when we are already feeling a little nervous.

Realistically, most interactions have many more touchpoints than we realise. Each of these touchpoints combine to create our overall feeling about the experience we have. Think of them adding up and giving the experience a score out of a hundred.

Now we need to start with the high-value touchpoints and do whatever we can to make each experience the best it can possibly be. Specifically, make the move from a simple transaction to a meaningful experience at every step – mostly this means doing smart little things, and these are generally the things your competitors won't do.

If you want another way to look at what we want to do with these touchpoints, think about the word 'ceremony', as in look for ways to create ceremony. Make moments special, look for ways to acknowledge them, create something unique around them. If we create a pile of little ceremonies for our customers, however we can, they will most certainly sit up and take notice.

Just remember two simple thoughts: transactions bad, experiences good.

STEP #9. Be prepared to let everything old go. Make room for everything NEW.

When we've spent a long time, often years, hanging onto a belief, it's often very hard to let go of it.

So what are the things we need to let go?

1. Our old thinking and limiting beliefs that no longer serve us

We need to let go of the old thinking, the limiting thinking, the low self-worth thinking, the truth (which isn't actually true), all the thoughts that keep us living with a small business poverty mentality. Letting go of this thinking doesn't happen easily; you will need to work on it every day. You are transforming your business – it starts with transforming your thinking.

2. We have to let go of the customers that we need to move on from

I have absolutely no doubt that as you move into the space of being the most expensive, or even simply starting to charge what you are worth, that you will lose some customers along the way. When I transitioned my marketing company I literally lost all of my clients. Why? Because I needed to. They were all nice people, but they wanted advice that they weren't really prepared to act on or to pay for. I had to let them go. And as I mentioned, I found myself in a flash and very expensive office, with no clients, a big bill – and a pile of fear. But I have absolutely no doubt I needed to let them go to become the business I wanted to be.

3. We need to let go of the staff who can't work in the new business

And make no mistake, it is a new business we are talking about making here. Not all members of your team will make the transition, because just as we get comfortable with the poverty-based business, so do our staff, and change and enlightenment both come slowly. Even back when I transformed my dive shop I lost some staff, but I soon attracted a much higher calibre of staff who were far more comfortable in the boutique style of shop and school that I was now running. And I see this happening more and more – quality people want to work for a quality business.

4. We need to let go of our old marketing messages

We can't transform our business and keep selling the old business. We need to start again with our messaging, we need to rethink our communication and what we need to say, and the stories we want to share and the discussion around the products and services we sell. As a friend of mine said, you can't sell a Ferrari the same way that you sell a Holden.

5. We have to let go of worrying what our competitors will think

Interestingly, this is a bit of a battle for some people. They are concerned about how their competitors will interpret this new business positioning. Personally I never cared, but it's a comment that has come up a number of times when I'm working with businesses to help them make the change. Focus on your business, not on your competitors.

6. Let go of the fear

This means letting go of the fear of this transformation not working. Is your business really working in its current state? Or is it anywhere close to working how you want it to be working? Probably not, otherwise you wouldn't be reading this book. We need to stop living in fear of the *what if?* What if this doesn't work? But what if it does? Turn the fear into excitement, passion and energy. Focus on the compelling future you are creating. One of the things I really do notice is that the longer the struggle has been for a business owner, the more their passion and energy has been whittled away. And you can't build a truly successful business without both.

Once we let go of all these anchors that are in so many ways holding us back, we can actually start to move forward. And rest assured, you will get tugged back into all these fears, limiting beliefs and negative thoughts often. Stay focused on the future. Deal with facts, not fiction every step of the way.

STEP #10. Stay on the PATH.

You've heard me say time and time again that heading down this path is not for the faint-hearted – it will take courage, it will take grit. In fact, it's been the single most common point throughout the book, and rest assured I'm not done yet.

Part XII is all about the need to follow through with the process and stay on the path. But right here, right now, I just want you to be clear that you will be tested and find it challenging when you make the decision to charge what you are worth and to be the best at what you do. If you can make it, you will never look back. So go into the process with your eyes wide open.

From my own personal experience and having worked with many other business owners to help them make the transition, there was a lot of fear at almost every step. The urge is always there to run back to lowering prices, to sell by cost and cost alone. To go back to the familiar, the old comfort zone, but that's what kept us there. And these feelings come up especially when you start to lose some old clients as you transition to the new business that you are becoming. Stay true to the path you have chosen.

This is a simple, 10-step process that isn't really that simple, but it gives you a path to follow. It works. I've seen it work many times, but you can't half do it. You are either in or out.

Now, a question I often get asked is, how long does this transition take? In reality, for me it was probably a six-month process when I look at it in detail. I had certain elements that I couldn't change in a hurry (a lease on my old office for one, and the negotiation of a new lease). But once I was committed to making the change, all the gears were put into motion and I never looked back.

NOW IT'S TIME TO RETHINK WHAT WE SAY

The only people who don't have imposter syndrome are the people who should.

Where are you now on your road to becoming the most expensive?

PART I: The BIG why ...

PART II: The world has changed – have you?

PART III: There are many very good reasons to be the most expensive

PART IV: How scared does this idea make you?

PART V: So what does it actually mean to be the best?

PART VI: Does this concept really work for any kind of business in any market?

PART VII: Surely the online world is completely different? Or is it?

PART VIII: Now we are convinced of the reasoning, we need some rules to work with

PART IX: The process we need to follow

PART X: Now it's time to rethink what we say

PART XI: More ways to increase your credibility, trustworthiness and 'buyability'

Part XII: This road is not for the faint of heart

IN THE LAST PART I spoke about the need to change our thinking, to be bold, to avoid simply trying to put lipstick on a wombat when it comes to repositioning ourselves and our business. While we need to change a lot to create this new, higher value, more expensive, charging-what-you-are-worth kind of business, in terms of creating experiences, committing to a culture of being the best and lots more, we also need to change how we sell ourselves.

This becomes increasingly important when you've been selling your products and services purely on price for a long time. I'm going to ask you to completely change the way you sell and the way you talk about your business, and that's not going to happen overnight. It's hard not to slip back into nasty old habits, but if you really are committed to changing your business, you're going to embrace this section.

I know that some of the ideas I'm going to suggest may feel a little challenging. I've spoken to enough audiences around the world and helped enough business owners to change their business model to charge what they are worth, and the biggest battle is not the physical stuff, it's the mental stuff. The way we talk about our business now, the stories we tell, the way we sell. It might take a little while to get there, but before long you'll stop having conversations about price and start having conversations about value. And that's when everything falls into place.

41

If you don't change your language it's unlikely that much else will change

How much is your language costing you every year?

We can go to a great deal of trouble to change everything in our business to really reposition what we do and to move from a business with a poverty mentality to one of abundance, but if we don't change the language we use, on the inside and the outside, it could all amount to nothing.

We've touched on the concepts of limiting beliefs and poverty mentality. Both of these are nurtured by our internal self-talk. What negative messages are we sending, what negative money issues are we reinforcing and creating by the language we use with ourselves in those quiet moments when we are left to our thoughts? Rest assured, I understand that language. The 'I'm not good enough' conversation, the 'no one will pay that much for what I'm selling'. The 'lack of' conversations, the 'imposter syndrome' conversations, the 'things are never going to get easier' conversations. We have to put a stop to all of them. But they are powerful words, and in most instances words we've been using for many years, and probably words our parents used.

If you want an abundant life, be abundant with others

I have developed an abundance mindset. I have rituals where I open my arms wide, close my eyes and welcome abundance of every kind into my life. I do this often throughout the day, and especially when times are getting tough. If you open my notepad you will find the word 'abundance' repeated everywhere. I welcome all kinds of abundance, from money to health, to love, to good people, to fun, to happiness. I choose my mood and refuse to play the victim, especially at times when money might not be flowing as freely.

I am a very big believer that much of our success or failure is tied into our mental approach, our day-to-day attitude and the way we live life. If you want an abundant life, be abundant with others. If you want more money, give more money. Don't hoard your every cent and be mean. If you want more love, be more loving. If you want to feel more supported, be more supportive.

Now I know that when you're reading a business book and we cross into the realms of personal growth, positive affirmations and inspirational-type messages, the hardcore business book junkies tend to do an eye roll. I get it. But believe me, of all my worldly experiences with entrepreneurs in every corner of this planet, the most successful ones, the ones with the greatest lives and the most financially successful ones, all share one thing – an incredible attitude of generosity and kindness and a warm and welcoming attitude of abundance. They give as much as they get in every way.

So what does this have to do with language? How can we become the most expensive? How can we charge more by simply changing our words? Well, if we don't change our words, we won't change anything.

Are you one of those folks who would feel uncomfortable being wealthy? Many people are. Deep down, do you resent rich people? Do you have bad associations around money from a childhood lived in poverty? It's OK – most of us have some of these issues. If we do, we need to reframe them. And that takes a great deal of inner talk.

Are rich people bad? Of course not. If you're worried about that, tell yourself a better story. I bet you love to help others. I absolutely guarantee that you'd like to help those closest to you financially, and maybe there are charities and other great causes you would like to support but you can't because you simply don't make enough money. Imagine if you were wealthy enough to help them. Imagine the good you could do with the money you make.

Reframe your thoughts.

For every negative thought you might have, reframe it. Come up with a better story. Tell it over and over again until you actually believe it.

I don't talk a great deal about my philanthropic activity, because I'm a pretty private person. But about five years ago, I came across an incredible lady doing everything she could to save wombats. She had set up a sanctuary called Sleepy Burrows. Donna is her name, and in my eyes she, and her husband Phil and her kids, are saints. When I first met them they were saving wombats that had been run over, shot, set on fire for 'fun', poisoned, were sick with a wombat parasitic condition called mange, kept as pets and mistreated, orphaned and so on.

The conditions of these wombats broke my heart, but the selfless and caring nature of this family restored my faith in humanity. Pretty much every penny that Donna and Phil made went to feeding the wombats they were caring for, building shelters and burrows, and buying medical supplies. And it was nowhere near enough.

I immediately wanted to help, and there were two ways that I could. Firstly, I could spread the word about the work being done to save these beautiful Australian animals, and secondly I could help them financially, which I do, every single month. Over the years, I've donated tens of thousands of dollars, and I'll keep donating till the day I die and even *after* that because I'm leaving money to Sleepy Burrows in my will.

Whenever I have those moments where I feel a little weird about charging what I'm worth, or about amassing a nest egg, I think about the good I'm able to do, and that gives me a very good reason to be OK with it. When I visit Sleepy Burrows, my heart is filled with so much love and respect, knowing that I've made a big difference to not only the wombats but also to Phil and Donna (and by the way, Donna received an Order of Australia award for her work protecting and rehabilitating wombats in NSW).

Now, that's just the wombats. I have other causes, mostly animal related. But I also grew up as an orphan, and I had all kinds of abuse to deal with in the first 15 years of my life. So I have a soft spot for kids in need. Again, through the Abused Child Trust, or ACT for Kids, an organisation that I'm an Ambassador for, I can use my powers for good!

I think you see what I'm saying. Reframe your negative beliefs, change the language you use, and think about what a richer version of you could do. And from experience, people who have grown up with little, and have struggled for a large part of their life, are often the kindest and most generous when they have money. They are good people.

The miserable bastards club is always recruiting

So yes, watch those internal discussions, the ones that fuel our limiting beliefs. At the same time, watch the language you use externally. How do you talk about your business, your clients, money? All of it. Do you do the 'being a small business owner is a constant battle', 'every day is a struggle', 'I haven't had a holiday in 20 years', 'poor, poor me' conversations with others? They need to end now.

Pull yourself up. Stop hanging out with other people who start these conversations and who fuel these conversations. Have more conversations about what you have, the great things your business gives you, the freedom, the autonomy, the satisfaction, the interactions. Have better conversations.

There is a club out there, with chapters in every city. It's called the Miserable Bastards Club, and the bad news is they are recruiting – and they want you. You know what they are like; I'm sure you know some members of the Miserable Bastards Club. Within one minute of seeing them the conversation has turned negative (normally, it takes less than a minute). You didn't realise how bad everything was until you started to speak with them. For the love of all things good, do everything you can to keep these people out of your life, because you will never achieve what I'm trying to help you achieve if the people around you are card-carrying members of the Miserable Bastards Club.

The place to start when it comes to our language is getting rid of the nasty, negative self-talk that has been holding us in a poverty space for a long time. This is the internal language and the external language. Spend more time around abundant people who never seem to have a lack of anything and listen to their language and the conversations they have. Do more of these things and the transformation of your business will be far more likely to succeed.

42

The single biggest marketing mistake that is more common than ever

We are really good at telling potential customers how we are exactly the same as our competitors, not how we are different.

The single biggest marketing mistake I encounter today is quite simply the fact that we go to great lengths to tell prospective customers how we are exactly the same as our competitors, not how we are different. This is because most businesses talk about themselves in terms of the products or services they offer, which they think define them. Or they use nebulous and, to be honest, beige statements like: 'the best service', 'you can trust us', 'the most convenient', 'the oldest' and – shock, horror – 'the cheapest'.

If you look at 10 accountants' websites they will basically all say the exact same thing. They state the obvious (they do tax), they make it all about their services (which are the same as their competitors), and they throw in a series of platitudes about service, how important the customer is and their commitment to you. The same applies to virtually every industry.

Visit pretty much any hotel website and there will be the same pictures of rooms, a pool, a buffet, a restaurant and a smiling face at check-in. Change the logo at the top of the page and you could be describing any hotel, anywhere.

I'm not just targeting accountants and hotels – every industry is the same. Lots of same, same, same and very little differentiation.

So, when we are basically offering the same kinds of products and services, how do we differentiate ourselves? A great question. And these are my thoughts:

1. Start by assuming that the customer knows the types of products and services your business sells. Don't treat them like they are idiots.

2. Create connection by showing that you understand their problems, challenges, hopes and expectations up front.

3. Share stories. Your stories, your customers' stories, your staff stories – stories, stories, stories.

4. Keep telling stories on a daily basis. Use social media for daily snapshots about who you are and how you can solve their problems. Build credibility by showing how you've solved similar problems for others in the same boat.

5. Look for ideas to market your business outside of your own industry. When an accountant is going to build a new website they will look at other accounting websites and actually list them in their brief to their website developer – 'we want our site to look like this'. I work with a lot of web developers and they say that this happens all day, every day.

Today, if you don't differentiate yourself from your competitors, you get stuck in the sea of beige, where everyone starts to look the same. It takes courage to differentiate, but when you are starting to position yourself as being the best, and being the most expensive, you had better get very good at it.

If you can't clearly show why you are the best, normally starting on your website, then there is no way anyone is going to buy anything from you when you increase your prices.

43

Really understand the role you play in solving problems for your customers

Give a man a fish and he eats for a day.
Teach a man to fish and he eats for a lifetime.
Teach a man to solve problems and he drives a Maserati.

I'm a giant fan of the book *Building a StoryBrand* by Donald Miller. It's a great book with a very powerful model to help business owners develop their messaging and their positioning by adopting a storytelling approach. There were two big realisations for me that I took from reading this book:

1. That in my story, my customers are the hero.

2. My role is to be the guide. To help them go from 'here' to 'there'.

Now this sounds so simple, and as always the best ideas generally are the most simple. But it was profound for me. I had always understood that when it comes to marketing ourselves, especially in the world of the 'expert' and 'influencer', we need to position ourselves as the authority and by association the hero of the story. But what Miller is suggesting is that our *customer* is the hero, and the hero has a problem.

What they actually want is a guide

Typically they want to go from where they are now to where they want to be, and they need someone to help them solve the problem that's preventing them from doing this. What they actually want is a guide. And they are looking for the best guide to suit their needs.

So, we have five things that we need to get crystal clear about:

1. Who the hero is (and by this I mean we have to clearly define our customer).

2. Know exactly where they are now and where they want to go.

3. Know exactly who or what the villain is in our hero's journey (what's stopping them?)

4. Understand that they are looking for a guide to take them from here to there.

5. Know what makes you the best guide for the job.

I liken this to standing at base camp in the Himalayas, and there is a man there who wants to climb Mt Everest and his sherpa hasn't turned up. There's a line of other potential sherpas who are available, but how is the hero in this story to decide? Does he go with the grizzly old veteran who has been up the mountain 50 times, or the young, strong sherpa who is packing drones and other tech to help with the climb?

When we are the guide, we need to make ourselves the most appealing guide that is relevant to the hero. Make sense? Buy the book. Get it on Audible if you want to listen to it immediately. It really helped me get clear on my role as a guide. And my mission is to be the most expensive guide, which means I have to be the best. And this applies to whatever it is I'm selling, to whomever the customer may be.

What are your customers' problems?

Businesses that really understand the problems their customers face, and that have the ability to show they understand these problems and provide a meaningful, compelling and totally value-based solution, are onto a winning formula.

And remember, the term 'problem' means vastly different things to different people. Insert whatever word you want to help get your head around it: challenge, opportunity, situation, drama, irritation and so on.

Think about how liquid paper came around. Nothing worse than making mistakes on documents and having to cross things out. Liquid paper provided a solution to an irritation; it didn't solve an earth-shattering disaster for an individual. (OK, it's not as relevant an issue as it was because no one seems to create hard copy documents anymore, but you get the point.)

One product that is solving a new problem is Soda Stream. You may have had a Soda Stream years ago. It was a simple way to make carbonated soft drinks from the comfort of your own home. They were popular for a while, but you had to buy the gas cartridges and the flavourings, mix them together, and then get that gas in there. It was all a bit of a bother, especially now when there are entire aisles dedicated to selling soft drinks. Soda Stream became far less relevant at solving anyone's problems, until now.

I was recently buying a juicer as a gift at an electrical appliance store and I saw a huge Soda Stream display. It seemed oddly out of context. I ask the sales guy what the story was, and he said they walk out the door now because people want carbonated drinks but they don't want to destroy the environment with single-use plastic bottles.

What I find wonderful about this is that a product that had become irrelevant suddenly found a new relevance as the problems of the customers changed.

As I've mentioned before, I help people to write books, specifically first-time authors. What's the problem I solve? To be honest, most people simply don't know where to start. And once they do start, they don't have a path to follow. As someone who has helped over 700 people to write their first books, I've clearly got a good system that anyone can follow, making me the best guide for the aspiring author. And I charge accordingly.

Anyway, I'm sure you get the drift. Spend time thinking about your customers – and the problems they have. But think deeper. There are surface problems and there are deeper problems or different desired outcomes. Think about the man who wants to lose 20kg. Does he *really* want to lose 20kg? Or does he want to find love by looking better in a pair of speedos, and feeling better and more confident in his own skin? Losing the 20kg is what he wants to do, the 20kg is the problem, but the outcome he wants is much bigger and far more meaningful than simply losing weight.

44

Think bigger – think globally – they will find you

If your business isn't growing it's dying – but growth means many things. The least meaningful relates to revenue.

One of the greatest things that I love about doing business these days is the sheer size of the opportunity we have because we live in such a digital and accessible world. It's becoming more common to have clients around the world, simply because we can communicate so easily and so cost effectively with platforms like Zoom.

But as much as it makes it easier for us to find customers and new markets, if we are smart at what we do, these new customers will find us. The constant and never-ending buzz of communication continues to rise exponentially every single day. This means that if we are good at what we do, and we are good at communicating our stories, there is a far greater chance of people finding us and buying from us.

Do you have a global market that you don't know about?

Now, I understand that not every business has a global market. But a surprising number do. And an even more surprising number probably do but they just can't move beyond thinking locally from a geographical point of view. So my first point is to think long and hard about what you are selling – and look for the reasons why people could and should be buying from you, as opposed to all the reasons why they should not.

My second point is that once we start to access a global market, we need to change our language, our stories and the narrative around our business and the products and services we sell. We have to make sure people know they can buy our products and services from anywhere on the planet, we need to sound bigger, more worldly, like dealing with people in Mongolia buying our products is really normal.

Think about the language you need to use when you are being global. Do you need translated websites to do business in Europe? What payment options will people want when it comes to buying internationally? How will you ship your products? Show that you are on top of these considerations.

When we start to think like a global business, regardless of whether we are a big business or a small business, we need to appear worldly. We must absolutely sell the uniqueness of where we are based, but we don't want to look too parochial.

45

Time to pull out the big guns – tell better stories

We live in a time when the stories we share are
part of the overall buying experience. Tell better stories –
be open, be honest, be transparent.

love storytelling. I'm a giant fan of using storytelling as a speaker
and as an entrepreneur. I've run storytelling workshops around the
world, I teach people to become better storytellers, and it's now
become an integral part of my coaching programmes. Storytelling
is incredibly powerful. I see so many examples of its significance in
the business world.

We want to buy from businesses that we have an emotional connection with, and this need is becoming more important every day.
We don't just want a meaningless interaction, we want engagement.
And our customers can get engagement if we share our stories and
let them into our business.

When we move to a model of being the most expensive, telling
our story well is imperative. The story needs to be told in a compelling way. And it's not just one story, it's a lot of stories, all woven
together. We need to tell the story of why we started the business,
the journey we've had, the ups and downs, what we got right and
what we got wrong, how we developed our products and services,
the stories of our team members, our customers, our industry, our
town. Stories, stories, stories.

I have absolutely zero doubt that if we tell the right stories, in the right way, we can transform into the business that is the most expensive. Of course, it's no good telling a big story if we don't deliver on our promise, but I'm making the assumption that you are absolutely committed to not just meeting your customers' expectations but exceeding them in every way.

Have you noticed the revolution in food descriptions? The more expensive the restaurant the more information we are given about the food we are being served. We are once again so much more aware and informed, and have access to more information, that we want to know as much as we can about the food we are eating.

Simply adding the word 'organic' means that whatever the food item is, it will have a premium price tag. We are told about the fish being line-caught, sustainably, from unpolluted waters. Or the beef being grown on Cape Grimm in Tasmania, a part of the world that has the cleanest and purest air in the world. We love to know as much as we can about our food – and this is now extending to many other types of products or services.

When a business tells their stories well, engagement is created. The customer experience becomes deeper and the perceived quality of the products and services increases. As does the value. The more we know, when it's delivered in a storytelling style, the more value we place on what we are buying – and if the value to us increases, we are prepared to pay more.

How much would you pay for tofu?

I'd like to share a story with you about tofu. Yes, that's right, good old tofu. Not something normally at the top of the menu. I was in Japan doing a study tour with a client; we'd been spending time researching everything from robotics to trees. It was very cool. One of the people who presented to our small group was the CEO of a large restaurant group that had 400 restaurants throughout Japan. They were very well known and respected for quality food. But they had struck a crossroad in the business and the future was looking somewhat uncertain for them.

Over the past few years they had noticed changing patterns with their customers, typically a younger market, mostly millennials. Everyone wanted their food faster, and they wanted to pay less for it. And this restaurant group felt that they had hit a wall.

They had done everything they could to speed up their service and to reduce costs so that they could offer a faster and cheaper product, but it never felt like their food was being served fast enough or cheap enough.

Did this mean they would have to change their model and become a fast-food restaurant? The idea mortified the business owners. They prided themselves on the incredible quality of the food they served, they had their own farms to grow the very best produce, they made their own tofu from the very best soy beans available – everything they did was about quality, and quality food takes time and costs money.

They had been successful for decades. Changing their business model was not something that they wanted to do, but maybe it was the only way they would survive?

After much debate and consideration, they decided to stand their ground. But they also decided it was time to do one thing very differently.

One of their bestselling menu items was a special tofu meal that they were very well known for. It was one of a handful of signature dishes, and it was very popular with their target market. Instead of reducing the price, they decided that they needed to tell a better story.

They set about telling the story of this tofu dish, the history behind growing the soy beans, their farms where all their produce is made, the age-old recipe that required the highest quality of ingredients and the time it took to prepare in a way they would be happy with. In other words, they made it very clear why the food takes time to prepare and why it will never be a cheap fast-food option.

They really understood that they were all about quality, and quite frankly if their customers weren't prepared to pay and to wait, they would rather shut the business down. A big statement.

They trained their thousands of staff to tell the story of the tofu, they put information all over the restaurant and made significant changes to their website. So what happened?

Once their customers were told the story of the tofu and the dish, in detail, they were actually more than happy to wait for it and to pay for it. They just needed to be told a better story, a more meaningful story that resonated with them. Once they were, no problem.

During the 12 months following this new storytelling initiative, their tofu sales, for that one dish, increased by thirty million dollars. This is a staggering result. And so, logically they started moving through their business and sharing stories about everything that they do, because they had worked out a very powerful modern-day marketing opportunity – don't be afraid to give your customers more information about your products and services. Just make sure it's relevant to them.

The different stories you should tell

So what are the stories we need to tell?

1. Our origin story – why we started this business.
2. Our history story – the hero's journey, the good, bad and ugly that led to today.
3. Stories about your products.
4. Stories about your services.
5. Stories about your people.
6. Stories about your customers.
7. Stories about your community.
8. Stories about updates, new products, and why they evolved.
9. Stories about what you do to give back to others.
10. Stories about your lessons along the way.
11. Stories about your dreams and where you are heading tomorrow.
12. Stories about your industry.

How many businesses would still be in business today if they learnt to tell a better story? Remember, our customers don't want to hear the sanitised, boring, predictable brochure-type story – they want the real stories, the warts and all stories, that show the real you. We are craving this level of authenticity and transparency, and smart, modern businesses are telling these stories so wonderfully well. Look around at new and contemporary businesses, in every space. See the stories, see the reinvention and reinvigoration that's happening across all industries. This is your opportunity to be a part of that.

And where do we want to tell these stories? EVERYWHERE. Simple as that. On your website, on your social media platforms, in your printed collateral, your advertising – EVERYWHERE.

If you want to be the most expensive, you need to share powerful stories that not only educate, but also inspire and engage your audience. Why do people want to buy a Maserati? Sure, it's a nice ego boost to drive around in a $250,000 car, but really, they are buying into the story and the history of Maserati, wonderfully told through the generations. They are buying a piece of history with all the cool that goes with it.

We live in a world where all we need to do to attract customers is to be brave enough, authentic enough and transparent enough to share the truth. Be who you are, not who you think your customers want you to be. Treat people with respect and they will reciprocate. And then, of course, you have to deliver on the promises that you make.

46

Help those around you understand your new business direction

We get tired of telling people about our business long before our customers get tired of hearing about it.

When we make some pretty major changes to our business, there has to be a transition period, and this is where the transforming takes place. But not everyone is going to get the new story and the new positioning straightaway.

One thing I noticed years back when I transformed my budget dive shop to a boutique dive school and retail showroom was that some of my old and loyal customers who were doing their best to stick with me and my new business model struggled to sell the new business. And as a result, they kept referring the wrong kind of customers to me, specifically the kind of customers I no longer wanted, as in the price-driven, budget-orientated kind.

I had to really go through a process of sitting down with these loyal customers and fans and thanking them for their referrals, but I had to explain to them my new business direction. I spoke about my vision for the future, my new philosophy about being the best and by association being the most expensive. I had to really spell out the type of customer I wanted to work with. These were often not easy conversations, because I saw the lights slowly going on as many of my existing loyal customers realised that they were probably not the customers I wanted, and that was a little awkward.

Like that moment when you walk into a bar and realise that this was a big mistake.

You are going to lose customers

Now when I'm helping my clients to transform their businesses, I place particular emphasis on the need to talk to your existing customers throughout your transformation. I mentioned earlier in the book that when you reposition yourself in the way I'm proposing, you are going to lose customers, and in fact that's a sign you are on the right path, no matter how scary it is. And yes, every business does lose some customers, but if we manage it well, we might keep more than we think, simply by engaging them in the transformation process.

To do this effectively means we probably need to have lots of one-to-one conversations during the transformation stage of charging what you are worth, explaining the reason for the shift (no one seems to like change), your vision and your plans for the future – and what this means for them. You basically have to sell them the concept of your new business and see how that sits for them. Do you keep them or do you lose them? Both outcomes are OK in my book.

What can happen though is that the business owner gets cold feet at this stage and reverts back to selling on price, being the cheapest and not making any money. So hold that resolve.

As soon as you are committed to transforming your business, start an educational campaign. Get your key messages right for your team, your current customers, your suppliers, your family, your friends, your community – everyone. Make sure you can tell the story of your new business concept in an authentic and engaging way.

The biggest point out of this is the old line – the 'what's in it for me?' As much as we would like to think everyone is deeply concerned and excited at the same time about our new business direction, what is probably most important to them is what impact it will have on them. And we need to be able to answer that.

The impact will of course vary, but in reality there will always be good things and bad things. Think about your team members.

I've noticed very interesting responses when I've transformed my business and others. When we start talking about the new direction that the business will be taking, these are typical responses:

The good things

- Staff get excited about the new direction.

- They like the idea of being part of the 'best' team.

- They understand value and the importance of the business being profitable.

- They assume it will lead to them making more money.

Their worries

- What if these changes don't work and the business goes broke?

- Will I be good enough to work in this new business?

- What happens to our existing customers?

- What will our competitors think?

- How much extra time will I have to put into upskilling?

- I like things the way they are now – what if I don't like the new business?

Now of course I'm generalising to a degree, but these are fairly typical responses that tend to come out over a period of weeks and months. If we know what the concerns may be, we can address them. If we know what the good things are that we are hoping to achieve, we can talk about them and get our team excited.

My point here is simple. Not everyone is going to be on board with our new business direction, and that's OK. But if we communicate our reasons, our intention, our strategy and our plan well, we are more likely to get a higher level of buy-in from those who matter the most. We need to think about this from every direction and how it will impact everyone. Then we can have the meaningful conversations accordingly.

47

The concept of 'subtle selling' – it's more powerful than you can imagine

Stop taking advice from backseat Uber experts whose only interest is selling you an overly complex product designed to build the business they want, not the business you want.

'm a giant fan of subtle selling, and personally, I'm finding that many of us are getting tired of the backseat Uber expert telling us that they have all of the answers and they will share them with us for the one-off, very low price of … surely we can do better than that?

Getting smarter with your selling

Subtle selling is where we incorporate and communicate what we do and the results we get in a much smarter way. Some may call it 'storyselling', others may call it subliminal selling. I don't really care what it's called, I just know it works.

Let me share an example with you. Let's assume I'm writing a book like this and I share an anecdote along the lines of:

Recently I met a man who made a point of coming up to me because he so desperately wanted to share his experience with small business poverty thinking.

This is a pretty self-explanatory kind of anecdote, but what if I added some more detail? Along the lines of:

Recently I was invited to present to 500 financial planners at a conference in New York City. As I finished the presentation to a round of applause, I was walking off the stage and I noticed a man looking intently at me, yet not coming over. I made a point of walking over to him, I shook his hand and mentioned that he looked like he had something to say ... would he like a chat?

Now this is the same story, just with some extra details added. But these details say a great deal about me:

1. That I'm a professional speaker.

2. That I was invited to speak in New York City, so I must be reasonably good.

3. I was speaking to a room full of professionals; that says a lot about the level of my content.

4. They were clapping when I finished, so I must have said something worthy of applause.

5. I noticed the man standing away from the stage, so I'm observant.

6. I went over to him and welcomed a chat, so I'm approachable.

That's a lot of extra information about me that just a few extra words have enabled. That's the reality of subtle selling. Share a little more information about the situation, the background, the reason, the story, and you not only make your example more interesting, you let people know more important information about you.

Now as you go through this book, I've made mention in a number of anecdotes and stories that I coach people, that I work with businesses, that I'm a speaker, that I'm experienced, that I'm passionate about what I do, and so much more. This extra information is genuinely part of my story, but it also lets you know much more about what I do without everything feeling like a sales pitch.

That's the key. Subtle selling is the way to educate potential and even existing clients about the products and services you sell, as well as what makes you different, your overall credibility and your personality – people can then decide if they would like to buy from you, or buy more. Have you gone to my website to find out more about me? Who I am and what I do? If you have, then perhaps my form of subtle selling has had an impact on you?

We can use subtle selling in our writing (think website, articles, social media), in videos, on podcasts – really anywhere you get the chance to share information about what you do with your target audience.

Another aspect of subtle selling I really like is that we can let our personality shine through, and we can also let our values and the things that are important to us to shine through. And today, that's what consumers want. We all want to know more about the people and the businesses we plan to spend money with. We want some transparency and some honesty – and as I've made mention of earlier in this part, we don't just want the Disney version, we want the whole story. The good, the bad and the ugly, as long as there is a happy ending (well … maybe we *do* want the Disney version).

48

You might want to find a quiet place and Google yourself

There's an old saying that goes something like this, 'you are who Google says you are', and that is more true than most of us would like to admit.

Having moved to Melbourne recently after living in Cairns for a very long time, one thing I've noticed is just how important online reviews are for just about everything in a capital city. Most people I know check out the Google reviews for a business before they invest time, energy and money into buying anything.

I'm not sure what's different in a regional area. Maybe being smaller means that we tend to ask for recommendations a little more. But without a doubt, when in the larger cities, online rating and referral platforms – things like Google reviews and Yelp – become our trusted advisors.

In the US, I found that Yelp was the go-to platform the last time I was there. In fact, I spent the weekend with some friends and our entire weekend of activities was planned around Yelp offers.

To me this means we have to make sure we are actively encouraging people to leave reviews, and the best way to do this is to ask them. But where possible, direct them as well. Try to encourage them to really follow your narrative about the quality, the experience, the attention to detail – and definitely not the price. The last thing we want are reviews saying you are the cheapest, because we know this will only encourage more cheap customers to head your way.

What are people saying about you?

So if you haven't done a Google search for your own business lately, maybe take a moment and do it now. Set up Google Alerts for you and your business (if you don't know how to do that or what it means, Google it). My point here is that it's important to know what people are saying about your business. There is no point going to the trouble and effort to completely transform your business to make it the most expensive if the online conversation about you doesn't align. Now this might take a little while to align, especially if you've had some issues with service delivery or the quality of your products in the past, but a lot of this comes back to having more honest and engaging communication with your customers. Or in other words, having better online conversations.

People are more accommodating of mistakes and issues if we handle them well, but you might need to look at doing some work to repair any damaged reputations. There are actually social media consultants that can help with this.

49

Become an incredible communicator

In the business world, exceptional communicators
can name their own price.

Now, I put this last, but it should almost be a section on it's own or, dare I say, a whole other book. One of the things that can really differentiate a business is the quality of its communication with its customers.

I was asked to do a keynote presentation to a few thousand mortgage brokers in Sydney. The topic was trust, specifically: how do they build trust with their clients to build stronger businesses? The client gave me a pile of information and statistics about what an amazing job they were all doing and how incredible their service was and so on. Yet something didn't seem to stack up for me. If they were all that good, why did they need me barking at them for an hour on some stage?

So I decided to do my own homework. I reached out to my community on social media and I asked them, 'For those of you who have used a mortgage broker, what did you love about what they did? And what was your biggest issue with your broker?' I asked a few more questions around this; to be honest I can't quite recall what they were and they don't matter. Within a day I had over 400 responses – and ninety percent of the respondents said that without a doubt their biggest issue was that their mortgage broker was terrible at communicating. The client has to constantly chase the broker.

Now when you get a response this compelling, you've got both your problem clearly identified and your opportunity. So I prepared my presentation, headed to Sydney a few weeks later, got on the stage, and said that if you want to dramatically improve your business learn how to return a phone call. Of course, they all laughed and acted a little superior, till I showed them the results of my survey, which was very hard to argue with. But, of course someone tried.

It starts with picking up the phone

A lady at the front of the room put up her hand to ask a question – and she blurted out, 'But what if we don't have anything to tell the client? We are waiting for the bank to get back to us?' And there was a chorus of agreement at this difficult situation that they found themselves in. My response was very simple: I said you ring the client to tell them that there is no news but you're onto it. That's really all the client wants to know. That you've got this covered and they can take it off their long list of things to worry about today, because they trust you to manage it.

Now this was surprisingly profound for these mortgage brokers. I'm not sure many of them got it, but I've received an email from a surprising number since who did adopt this simple strategy and on average their word-of-mouth referrals had increased by somewhere between thirty and fifty percent. The power of communication.

The same applies to just about any business in just about any industry. Set a goal to become an extraordinary communicator and your business will already be way out in front of most of your competitors. Not that hard really. But we all get busy, we are all juggling so many things, that – strangely – communicating with our customers becomes a low priority. I know, I'm incredibly busy with a to-do list that goes down my desk, across the floor and out the door. I need to keep reminding myself to get better at this too.

Interestingly, my publisher for this book is a company called Publish Central. The founder is a man called Michael Hanrahan, and I don't think I've ever met anyone as good on the phone as him. Now, I've recommended so many authors to this company over about seven or eight years, and I've never had a single complaint or issue from anyone I've recommended to Publish Central. That is astonishing. Publishing is a complex process with plenty of room for error; egos can get a little hurt and deadlines do blow out. Every single person raves about Michael and his partner Anna. And the number one compliment? The extraordinary level of communication that comes from this company. Oh, and by the way, Publish Central is the most expensive publisher and they are certainly the best. Mmmmmm, makes you wonder, doesn't it?

Anyway, I'm sure you get the drift. You might have the best products or services, but if your communication sucks, the whole thing can fall apart at the seams. It's something we have to work at. But in reality, it's not that hard.

Part XI

MORE WAYS TO INCREASE YOUR CREDIBILITY, TRUSTWORTHINESS AND 'BUYABILITY'

Your reputation is the single biggest asset
your business has. Protect it all all costs.

Where are you now on your road to becoming the most expensive?

PART I: The BIG why ...

PART II: The world has changed — have you?

PART III: There are many very good reasons to be the most expensive

PART IV: How scared does this idea make you?

PART V: So what does it actually mean to be the best?

PART VI: Does this concept really work for any kind of business in any market?

PART VII: Surely the online world is completely different? Or is it?

PART VIII: Now we are convinced of the reasoning, we need some rules to work with

PART IX: The process we need to follow

PART X: Now it's time to rethink what we say

PART XI: More ways to increase your credibility, trustworthiness and 'buyability'

Part XII: This road is not for the faint of heart

WE'VE SPENT A LOT OF TIME getting clear on the concept of charging what you are worth and the relationship between this and offering exceptional quality products and services, exceeding your customers' expectations and then taking a systematic and strategic approach to actually starting to increase your prices, with the end goal of being the most expensive in your space. So we've covered a lot of ground. I'd now like to spend time looking at the icing on the cake, and that is credibility.

If you're keen to get cracking on the strategies I've introduced, even though some parts may feel a little scary, there is another giant leap and huge opportunity to really take your business to the next level of success by increasing your credibility in the marketplace. The more credibility you have, the easier it is to charge what you are worth and the more customers will miraculously find their way to you – and these are the right customers, the ones we really want.

I've spent a lifetime building my personal brand – it's my most prized asset in many ways. I've always acted with the highest of integrity. Maintaining my reputation as an ethical entrepreneur has and continues to be hugely important to me. And it pays off. If you build a reputation for integrity, for being good at what you do (in fact, being *great* at what you do), being ethical and honest, and for always exceeding your customers' expectations, you'll end up being one of those businesses that others rave about. And we all want that.

If you want another word to use alongside credibility, let's add the word *trust*. There is a major trust deficit out there at the moment – it really started during the Global Financial Crisis and it hasn't got much better in the subsequent decade. If you don't actively work to build trust, your customers will find someone who does. Of course, trust can take many years to build and it can be destroyed in a second with one stupid action, one stupid post and certainly one stupid comment.

This section is really all about ways to show your credibility, to build your level of trustworthiness with your customers and your overall 'buyablity'.

50

Write a great book that solves people's problems

Content is currency and a book is the
greatest piece of content there is.

O K, as an author I have to say that writing a book is a good
thing. I get that. For me though it has been transformational
to say the least. I wrote my first book over 20 years ago.

I'm a commercial diver by trade. As I've mentioned, my first
business was a SCUBA school and retail shop I purchased when
I was 18. I also recovered boats that had sunk and did other commercial work for many years. On one job that I was doing on the
Great Barrier Reef, installing a pontoon for helicopters to land,
I got a bad case of decompression sickness. After a six-month recu-
peration, I was told by my neurologist that I would never be able
to dive again. Those pesky little nitrogen bubbles had done way too
much damage throughout my body.

At the time I was working for a Japanese shipping company.
They suggested I join their sales team, and after a few transitional
problems, I took to it like a duck to water. From there, I travelled
the world for five years promoting the cruises on Australia's Great
Barrier Reef.

Then I started a small marketing company. I noticed that most
small business clients had the same kinds of problems, and I was
answering the same questions all day long. To make matters worse,

these businesses were telling me their problems, asking me for help, and then casually letting me know that they had no money to pay for my advice. Basically I was running a not-for-profit business (sound familiar?).

So I developed a pile of fact sheets that answered the most common questions I was being asked. To me this was a way to save time and money. If someone called up with a problem and didn't have any money for professional advice, they were welcome to come into my office and collect some simple 'how to' information. We had copies of about fifty of these sheets on the wall in my office.

Then I had the idea to write another fifty, put them together and make it a book called *101 Ways to Market Your Business*. I had a contact in the publishing world who showed it to an editor, who in turn forwarded it to a friend of theirs, and lo and behold, I was offered a publishing contract. I was very fortunate – my first book was published by one of the great publishers in Australia, Allen & Unwin, and it was extraordinarily successful. This was the start of my publishing world, and I published a further 11 books with Allen & Unwin and one with Simon & Schuster. Now I self-publish.

Everything changed with my first book

To say my first book transformed my life is the biggest understatement I could make. Everything changed. I started to get featured in the media, I was asked to speak at conferences and events, I had clients coming out of the woodwork, and they expected to pay rates far higher than I had been charging. The credibility of this, my first book, really sparked a massive change in my life and in my thinking. And my book was simple; it was a book of ideas to help small business owners make more money. And ironically, here I am doing it again with book number 14.

Today one of the services I offer is helping people to write their first book. I've helped many new authors write non-fiction books and they have all gone on to use these books to build their credibility and their businesses. A book is basically a business card on steroids. The books that are the most successful are the ones that solve other people's problems. None of my books are about splitting the atom – they provide simple, practical advice, based on my own experience.

Now, I'm also going to add a little clause in here, simply because it's something that is important to me and having helped over seven hundred first-time authors to write a book, around the world, it needs to be said. I don't just encourage people to write any old book, I encourage and teach them to write a quality book, one that they will be proud of, one that will build and enhance their credibility and one that will garner the respect of their audience. There are a lot of author coaches out there saying things like:

- 'Don't worry about your content, just write anything, no one reads it anyway. It's just to say you've written a book.'

- 'You can write a book in 48 hours.'

- 'Don't worry about printing it, an ebook is all you need.'

- 'Don't go to the expense of getting it professionally published.'

These and lots of other statements get thrown around when it comes to writing and publishing a book. This entire book and premise is about quality. Simple as that. I've used books to build a global business over the past 20 years, my clients include the likes of the European Union, CBS, Hewlett Packard and hundreds more. Why? Because I've built a world-class reputation. That doesn't happen if you simply churn out any old book, get it printed at Officeworks and call yourself an author.

What's my point? Engage a decent book writing coach (beware of the dodgy ones – the bigger their offer and promise the shonkier they tend to be), invest the time and energy to write a world-class book, pay the money and get it professionally published at the highest standards and use your book as your brand building credibility tool.

I'll put my soapbox away for now.

51

Be brave and get on some stages

The key to a great presentation is to make the audience laugh, make them cry and make them think.

've been a speaker in various guises all of my working life. I actually did Toastmasters training when I was about 15 years old. At the time it was just to get out of doing other schoolwork, but it kind of stuck with me. If you get up on a stage in front of others and share your knowledge, your experiences and your story, you will most definitely grow and become more credible.

The opportunities and the credibility that come from speaking are incredible, and just as powerful as writing a book, but in reality, the book is what gets us onto the stage. When I look back at my speaking career to date, I've delivered over 500 presentations in 25 countries and worked with clients as big and bold as the European Union, Hewlett Packard and Hertz, right down to smaller, unique and equally as extraordinary organisations. I've done a TEDx talk called 'Imagine if we were 33% less angry', and had the great pleasure of working with people including Richard Branson, Tim Ferriss and many others. Imagine the credibility that this gives me.

You can learn to be a better public speaker

Now I know that many people find public speaking really scary. I completely understand. No one wants to look like an idiot in front of a room full of strangers, or even worse, a room full of people we know. But like most things, it's all about learning some skills and being taught how to overcome nerves, develop a little stage craft, create audience engagement and so on. Most importantly, before you get on stage, make sure you have something to say.

When I first started speaking, it was at local business events, chambers of commerce functions, training programmes, company retreats, things like that. Typically I was asked to share my story as an entrepreneur. What had I learned along the way? What were my challenges? What solutions did I work out? People are fascinated by stories, and no matter what you think, you have an interesting story that others want to hear.

It's not about being the greatest speaker of all time. It's about getting up and being honest and authentic. It's about telling your story, warts and all, and doing it to help those in the audience. If you approach speaking to a group from this angle, I think it becomes much easier.

Get some training. I'll do a shameless plug here for my speaker training. I work with beginners through to veterans. Go to my web-site and find out how I can help. Or go online and find the local Toastmasters Chapter – they have all kinds of simple and affordable speaker training programmes on offer.

And if you're one of those people who thinks they have nothing of value to share, I assure you that you are wrong. Everyone has great value in what they have experienced and learned along the way, and by sharing it you might just help someone else. In fact, you might help a whole lot of people. No one else on the planet has had the same experiences, challenges, realisations, learnings or bazinga moments as you. Your unique life is of immense value to others.

If you're brave enough to get up on a stage, and there are always opportunities to do this, and you can share your story and how you got to where you are today in a very down-to-earth and authentic way, your credibility will grow dramatically.

52

Work with better quality partners

If you lay down with dogs you get up with fleas.
So either buy a flea collar or find better quality partners.

Our credibility can be dramatically impacted in good ways and bad ways by the people we work with. The organisations we partner with say a lot about us, and because of this we need to think long and hard about the brands we want to be associated with.

I'm not going to say a lot about this — it's really pretty self-explanatory. Before working with an organisation or an individual, it pays to ask ourselves if this is good for our brand and for our credibility. If it's not, no matter how tempted you might be because of the money, walk away.

There are certainly organisations I would not work for, no matter how much they paid me. And the same applies to certain individuals. I've worked too hard to build my credibility over many years to throw it away by partnering with a dodgy company or person.

Now, you have to determine what dodgy means to you. For me it means we don't have the same values. It means they lack integrity as I see it. Will people look at me and my brand disparagingly as a result of me working with this particular person or organisation?

If you have any doubts about whether or not you should work with or partner in some way with a person or an organisation, you've probably got your answer there. Listen to your gut instinct – it won't lead you astray. At the same time, do your homework. A lot can be revealed about an individual or an organisation with a simple online search. Be slow to partner; don't get pressured into rushing into something until you've had the time to do your research. And once again, if you have the slightest doubt, and I do mean the slightest, run.

53

Collect as many 'trust logos' as possible

If you don't give people a reason to trust you, they won't.

What exactly are trust logos? If you go to my website (www.andrewgriffiths.com.au) you will see logos from the companies I've worked with, the media I've been featured in and the businesses I partner with. The implied message from these logos on my website is that I'm credible and to be trusted. They are testament to my integrity.

Of course, we can be a little cynical about trust logos; there is no shortage of people who have appeared trustworthy on the outside only to be found out at some stage for being anything from a drug cheat to a mass murderer. But let's just assume for the time being that you are trustworthy and you keep your mass murdering to a minimum.

Trust logos differentiate us, add to our overall credibility, and make us more trustworthy. Put them on your website if you can. But don't be dodgy about it. If you managed to get the business card of a CEO from a large company, but you haven't actually done any work for them, you can't put their logo on your website. Sounds obvious right – but you'd be surprised at how many people blur the edges of 'clients I've worked with'. My take on this is if I can't honestly justify using an organisation's logo, as in I've done some significant work for them, then I won't.

Another point to consider here is what to do if a company you have done work for – and you proudly promote the fact on your website and in your promotional material – goes and gets into trouble. What do you do? I suggest taking their logo off your site. Distance yourself as much as possible. Good organisations go bad, it's a part of life, just don't let your reputation get tarnished by their demise.

54

Don't underestimate the value of testimonials

Testimonials have always been important,
now they are essential.

'm a giant fan of testimonials. They have stood the test of time in our digital world. Testimonials provide a way for others to say nice things about us. The more of them we can use the better.

I do think it's good when asking for testimonials from clients to give them some direction. Let them know what you will be using the testimonial for, and what types of things you would like them to talk about. It all gets a little dull if every testimonial simply says you are awesome. We need a little more depth than that.

Some people struggle to ask their customers for testimonials. My advice is to make it easy for them. As mentioned, give them direction about the kind of testimonial you want. Ask for either written or video testimonials. Let them know where you are going to use them (on your website, on your social media, in your book). And be extremely grateful to them for doing so.

Having people post testimonials about you and what you do on social media simply because they proudly want to promote you is such a great feeling and if we are good at what we do, and we manage to really exceed expectations where we can, as often as we can, people will do exactly that.

One concerning trend these days is the rise of the fake testimonial, especially on third party sites. This is where people either set up a new email address, normally a gmail account or something similar and use it to write their own testimonials, or even worse, use it to bag their opposition. I can't believe that people do this, but they do.

Remember, total integrity in everything you do. Leave the fake stuff to the shonksters and if anyone suggests you should do this kind of thing because 'everyone does it', find new advisors as fast as you can.

Testimonials are powerful tools. Potential customers will believe what someone else says about our business far more than they will believe what we say about our business – so be aware of this. Work on your technique to encourage happy customers to tell the world about you and your business. Remember, no testimonials looks as bad as lousy testimonials.

55

The media is a powerful leveraging tool

The media is a machine that
needs credible people saying credible stuff
(and lots of people saying crazy stuff).

G etting media exposure is another great way to build credibility, assuming it's good media exposure, right? No one
wants to be featured on *A Current Affair* running out the
back door of their business with a towel wrapped around their
head and a cameraman chasing them up the road. But seriously ...
the media is always looking long and hard for good stories about
businesses doing things differently, overcoming challenges, bucking
trends, coming up with a new invention. And it really isn't that hard
to get media exposure.

I'm not going to go into a lot of detail here about working with
the media; that's not what this book is all about, but I'll offer a few
tips. If you think your business has a good story to tell, you could
look to engage a public relations firm to help you get some positive
exposure. At the same time, there are some great platforms that will
teach you how to do PR yourself. To be honest, it's not that hard.
Remember – the media needs stories to feed an ever-increasing
demand for news.

I've had the good fortune of being interviewed for radio shows,
TV shows, newspapers and podcasts – hundreds of times. The real

value comes from the exposure created, as well as the credibility I get from featuring these media interviews on my website. There is an inferred credibility when you see logos like ABC, Channel 7, *Australian Financial Review*, CBS and the like on a website.

The media need credible sources, and as the new world of media grows, think online, podcasts and new digital TV channels, let alone social media and so much more – they need good people to interview, to share their knowledge, their expertise and their stories. And that can only be good for business.

56

Create high-quality content on a regular basis and share it

Today, content is currency. You need to decide if you're dealing in pesos or pounds.

Content is a form of currency in the modern world, and there is no shortage of it. But at the same time, there is an ever-increasing demand for content of all kinds, from the trashy to the helpful. If you can create and share content – useful, high-quality and high-value content – your credibility will grow.

So what exactly is high-quality content? To me it's content that solves problems, provides useful advice, entertains, provokes thought, and encourages and inspires. Content can be in the form of articles, images, videos, tips, advice of all kinds, podcast shows – you name it. The key is making it useful – with whatever that may mean to your customers, both existing and potential.

If you can create great content, on a regular basis, and share it with a growing community via social media, you will develop a following, and this means more potential clients. People love to follow interesting businesses that are doing smart and innovative things.

57

Be careful what you post on social media

If you're going to do dumb things,
assume they will end up online.

I love social media. I'm not one of those people who bitch and moan and complain about what a waste of time it is, only to sneak off and spend hours trawling through it to see what everyone else is saying. I find it a positive space to share my thoughts, to support others and to make a difference. My community, my social media followers and fans are generally very positive and supportive of me, and to be honest, I don't really entertain a whole lot of negativity or trolling.

Social media can make us or break us

However, when it comes to credibility, social media can make us or break us. I'm noticing more and more clients who have gone back through my social media to check the types of posts I've made, the information I've shared and the comments I've made before they will commit to working with me. Why?

We all know our website is only going to say how awesome we are, right? Yes, it's absolutely essential and important, and it's going to have a lot of stuff about what we do and what we've done. But websites tend to be a bit static in that regard. Think of a hotel website – everything is awesome, right? Beautiful rooms, pools, restaurants, amazing staff, great meals.

But our social media is like our daily check-in. Social media is kind of like the pulse of our business. It's more real and relevant, sometimes a little gritty; it's where we say the things that we wouldn't talk about on our website. So, to use the hotel analogy, social media is a little more like Trip Advisor – others are talking about what the hotel is *actually like*, not what the nice website says – and they are sharing based on what they have experienced today.

So our website might say all the right things, but does our social media? We've recently seen comedian Kevin Hart get kicked out of hosting the Oscars because of a comment he made on Twitter almost 10 years ago. We've seen an American dentist forced into hiding after posting a picture of himself next to a lion he shot in Africa (this picture received close to 100 million views). There are so many examples of people basically destroying their reputations because of what they've posted on social media. And before people want to give us their hard-earned money, or in the case of corporates, before they get into trouble, everyone is looking a little closer at exactly who we are and what we believe in, and the best way they can do that today is through what we say on social media. Think long and hard about that.

I am extremely (and I mean *extremely*) considered with everything I post on social media. I know that my prospective and my existing clients will see it. I ask myself a few questions before I post anything:

1. Is this post helpful and/or of interest to my target market?

2. Is this post in alignment with my values?

3. Is this post appropriate for my brand?

4. Is there any chance of this post being interpreted in a negative way?

Bottom line: by all means post on social media – it's essential in my view – but be very considered and have your own guidelines to keep you out of harm's way.

58

Build an awesome website and keep it up to date

I'm flabbergasted at how many businesses
either have no website or a lousy website.
I'm not sure which is worse.

Well, this may seem kind of obvious to say, but it does
surprise me in this day and age that so many business
owners have lousy websites. There really is no excuse for
it. Now, I know elsewhere I've said that when you are the most
expensive at what you do, people have a way of tracking you down.
But just being the most expensive isn't always going to be enough
to seal the deal – and your website forms the silent sales tool that
does it.

A couple of years back I did a major website overhaul for my
products and services. This was a big project, because I do a lot of
things. I also knew that this website really needed to be different.
It was my third website in terms of a personal branding site (www.
andrewgriffiths.com.au) and it took quite a bit of time to really
think about what the message was that I wanted to send.

I worked with a wonderful friend, Sarah Powell, who helped me
to plan out the site. And through many conversations, I realised that
the one word that I wanted to come to mind when people visited
my new site was 'CREDIBILITY'. I wanted anyone who came to
my site to say to themselves, 'this guy's the real deal'. This meant that

my messaging, branding, storytelling, trust elements, products and every other element of the site had to reinforce my credibility.

It can't just look awesome – your website has to *work*

Now, the project was done and the new site launched, with fantastic feedback every step of the way. I was really proud of the job done by Sarah, my web developers – everyone involved. It looked awesome. But did it work? Did my brand new, hugely expensive website really hit the mark? It did – and I could tell that it did immediately by the types of emails I started to get, and continue to get today.

In the past, whenever someone emailed me about a speaker engagement, their only question tended to be 'how much do I charge?' But the enquiries were very different after launching my new site. They went more along the lines of the following:

> *Dear Mr Griffiths,*
>
> *In May 2021 we are putting on an event in San Francisco where we are getting global entrepreneurial thought leaders to present their best thinking to a group of business leaders from around the world. You would be perfect as a paid speaker for this event.*
>
> *We have two questions:*
>
> - *Does this event interest you?*
> - *Are you available to travel to San Francisco for an event on May 12?*
>
> *Kindest regards,*
>
> *Bill Smith.*
>
> *PS Can you also let me know your speaker fee and travel requirements to that I can budget accordingly?*

It's very easy to see that the second email is very different to the first email. What changed? My website. The messages I sent, the credibility I portrayed and, of course, the credibility I could deliver on.

So, how do you make a website that exudes credibility? Include everything I've spoken about in this book, and in particular in this section, along with a few other goodies:

1. Tell your story (written in the first person ideally), explain why you do what you do, how you do it, the challenges you've overcome and your mantra or overarching philosophy.

2. Have really good images of you and your products. And try not to make them too cliché. But if you're a great chef, we want to see pictures of you making food. If you're a great garden landscaper, we want to see pictures of you in a garden.

3. Have incredible testimonials from people. Make them considered, direct the testimonials, tell people what you want, get the messages out that address and identify all the reasons why yours is the go-to business in this space.

4. Put up the logos of those people who do business with you or who you've done business with. The bigger the brands the bigger the credibility.

5. If you've written a book or two, put that information on your site (and if you haven't written a book, write a book and then put it on your website).

6. Let your personality shine through on your site. Don't be afraid to be playful.

7. If you've had some media coverage, include that.

8. Have a decent and active blog. One article posted in 1998 is not an active blog.

9. Have direct links to social media. Your website tells everyone how awesome your business is but it's kind of static. Your social media is your daily check-in. It provides currency, news, what's happening, updates. It's where we feel the pulse of a business.

10. Make it really clear what you sell – and make it really easy for people to buy what you are selling.

Now, I'm taking it for granted that you'll use a good web developer and graphic designer – after all, the best information poorly presented kind of defeats the purpose. And I'm still a little blown away by the fact that up to fifty percent of small businesses in Australia don't have a web presence. That could also account for why so many small businesses go broke so early on in their history.

Part XII

THIS ROAD IS NOT FOR THE FAINT OF HEART

Never let the opportunity to make
a good decision float by.

Where are you now on your road to becoming the most expensive?

PART I: The BIG why ...

PART II: The world has changed – have you?

PART III: There are many very good reasons to be the most expensive

PART IV: How scared does this idea make you?

PART V: So what does it actually mean to be the best?

PART VI: Does this concept really work for any kind of business in any market?

PART VII: Surely the online world is completely different? Or is it?

PART VIII: Now we are convinced of the reasoning, we need some rules to work with

PART IX: The process we need to follow

PART X: Now it's time to rethink what we say

PART XI: More ways to increase your credibility, trustworthiness and 'buyability'

Part XII: This road is not for the faint of heart

I'VE BEEN VERY CLEAR about this point right from the beginning of this book. It's very easy to fall in love with the idea of being the business that charges the most and enjoying all the benefits that this brings, but from my experience, few people will have the courage to do what it takes to get here.

I'm not trying to be negative, I'm just calling it the way I see it. There are so many pitfalls along the way, making it really easy to get derailed. And this is not the kind of thing you can half do. You are either all in or all out.

So I've included this part as a last-ditch effort to really spell out how this will look and feel if you commit to going down this road. All I can promise is that if you do decide to be the most expensive and, by association, become the absolute best at what you do, your life will never be the same again.

59

Accept that a lot will change in your world – and change is never easy

*If you want to build a better business
start by building a better person.*

We've all been through periods of change before. Sometimes it's forced upon us, coming unexpectedly and causing a lot of emotional turmoil and pain. Other times we bring it on ourselves, and we experience a lot of emotional turmoil and pain. But most of us also know that to achieve anything worthwhile in life, it will take significant change, and we need to get ready for that.

The process I'm encouraging you to undertake is certainly one that will require a lot of things to change. It will need considerable investment of time, energy, money and more. It will be a risk and it will take time. It could be a process that makes or breaks you. The thing is, if what you're doing now, and what you've been doing for many years, isn't working, and has no signs of ever working, surely it's worth taking the risk for some radical change in your life?

Every time your heart misses a beat, or you get cold feet, just think back to a time when you've done something really hard. Think about how scary that was, how easy it would have been to have simply turned back, but you didn't. You forged ahead, regardless of how scared you were, and you did what needed to be done, and if you're anything like me, you're incredibly grateful today.

60

It might be scary at first, and business may drop while you change your customer mix

The more excuses you can find for why you can't do something right now the more important it is that you do it.

One of the things I've made mention of throughout this book is that a by-product of the process I'm promoting is that your customer base will, in all likelihood, change, and that will be scary.

It means that to get new customers, the right kind of customers, those who are prepared to pay for quality, your old price-driven customers will probably need to go. So the bottom line is, business will get worse before it gets better. But it will be worth it (hopefully I've made that part clear). This means if you start to notice that you are losing some of your old customers, take that as a good sign, albeit a slightly scary one.

I know that when I completely changed my marketing company from a poverty-based business to an abundant business, I had to make many changes which I've spoken about earlier. When I closed the doors to the old business, I literally had no customers to take with me to the new business. That was terrifying.

I remember sitting in my flash new office, looking around at how much money I had just spent, how uncomfortable but awesome everything felt, and slowly coming to terms with the fact that I didn't have a single customer to help pay the rent or the wages or the moving bill.

But as you read earlier, it didn't take me long to get an incredible customer base, even though my fees had increased by three hundred percent. I was working with banks, lawyers, accounting firms, architects, shopping centres, web developers – all high-quality clients who understood what it meant to pay for quality.

Your customer mix will change. But if you do this process correctly, it will change for the better, and you'll be asking yourself why you didn't do this years ago.

61

Your competitors might get a little dirty

'If you aren't upsetting a few people you're
not trying hard enough.'
Seth Godin

An interesting thing can happen when you stop competing with your competitors, and simply move out of their league – they might not like it and this might mean they start to act out.

Before I transformed my marketing business, it seemed that everyone was my competitor. And in reality they were. We all under-charged the same amount, we were all fighting for the exact same customers. When you think about it, it's stupid. As soon as I adopted my 'be the most expensive' attitude and started to make changes, wrote a book on marketing, became a speaker on marketing and everything else, I noticed a certain shift in the relationship between myself and the other companies.

Those businesses that were really good at what they did, the ones that never accepted me before, now did so. They reached out, almost welcoming me into the fold of professionals. It was a nice feeling to be respected, and even as I outgrew them in terms of size and capability, there was always a professional respect.

Whereas the competitors I felt that I had outgrown, simply by making the moves I did, in many ways they became bitter and resentful (or just *more* bitter and resentful), and most are still doing exactly the same work for the same clients as they were 25 years ago – and making the same amount of money, zero.

Simply understand that not everyone wants to see you blossom in your business. That's OK, it's human nature. Just keep your eye on the ball.

62

You have to stay focused on the benefits of being the most expensive

Keep reminding yourself daily why you are doing this and one day you won't need to.

One piece of advice that I think is really helpful is that you need to stay focused on the benefits of being the most expensive. What would it mean to you and your family if your business stopped being run with a poverty mentality and started being run in a way that generated the right profits, that attracted the right kinds of loyal customers and that was in many ways so much less stressful to run?

If you're at the end of your tether in terms of running a business with one strategy – be the cheapest – or even if you haven't consciously set out to be a poverty mentality business (let's be honest, who does?) and instead you've simply ended up here, this is when we tend to have all the motivation we could ever want.

We are simply sick and tired of chasing our tail, never having any money in the bank and always feeling underappreciated by our clients. You probably have all the motivation you need to make some significant changes, starting with what you charge.

I'd suggest making a list of the benefits this new direction will bring to your life. Be specific with the details. Stay focused on what you are trying to achieve and how this will be your big 'WHY?' Something we all need.

63

You will probably need NEW – new staff, new advisors, new friends

If we don't embrace new, we get old surprisingly fast.

As you change, as your business changes, as you start to see what a quality business and a quality attitude can do for you, you may find that your existing staff need to lift to their game – and I hate to be so blunt (I don't really), but some of them will probably need to go. Not everyone can deal with the type of change I'm suggesting, and if you're not careful, you might find yourself with a few saboteurs in there, keen to make sure things don't work.

Who will make the leap with you?

Now I'm sure you are thinking I'm being paranoid. Actually, I'm not. I've experienced this firsthand on several occasions, when I've made the transition from being a poverty-thinking business to a 'charge what I'm worth' kind of business. Some of my team simply couldn't make that leap with me and they had to go before their negative attitude sunk the ship. And I'm going to emphasise a point here: never, ever underestimate the damage one staff member with the wrong attitude can do.

When I'm working with a business to help them make this transition, I go to great lengths to talk to every member of the team, one on one, in private, to get a clear understanding of who is on board and who is not. While I'll give anyone a chance to get with the programme, I give them a very specific timeframe for that change in attitude to appear, and if I have my doubts, they are gone.

The same concept applies to our advisors. Is your current accountant going to give you the advice you need with this new approach? To be honest, if they haven't pointed out that you are grossly undercharging, you need a new accountant anyway. Look at your advisors: are they prosperous, successful, and do they charge accordingly? With your new state of mind and state of doing business, you need like-minded advisors to give you the right advice, not poverty-mentality advice.

Last but not least, the people we spend time with, our business associates who are probably classified as friends, may end up changing. Poverty mentality in business attracts other business owners with the same issue. If you want to be truly financially successful, find financially successful people and spend time with them.

Think of the analogy of losing weight. How likely are you to lose that 20kg if the people you spend most of your time with are overweight, don't exercise, eat badly and never, ever hold you to account to act better or to encourage you to lose that 20kg. But if you are 20kg overweight and you start hanging out with people who exercise daily, eat well, do active things on the weekends and generally live in a healthy way, the 20kg will disappear almost by itself.

The same applies with making money, having self-worth and self-value. Hang with the right people and you are halfway there. Now, please don't get me wrong; I'm not about getting rid of loyal friends in favour of some flashy, gold-chain-loving, sports-car-driving, shallow jerk who only cares about money. There is a big difference between that kind of person and someone of substance, who is financially successful in their business, and committed to their community, their family, their customers and their industry.

What I'm saying is that if you keep all the same people in your world who have supported your poverty mentality and overall state of mind until now, it's very unlikely that much will in fact change. I know this is tough, but you either want to change or you don't. You might be surprised by who actually comes along for the ride and who is the most supportive and able to evolve.

64

You can't do this a little bit – all in or all out … there is no middle ground

You don't have to change the world,
just change your world.

This feels like the logical place to end this book. Stepping up and actually charging what you are worth, and even better, doing everything that it takes to become the most expensive in your space, is not something you can half do. Many have tried, few have succeeded. This is an all-in or all-out kind of activity.

I've got no doubt that in many ways I've made it sound simple, but I've also done my best to be absolutely clear that this is not for the faint of heart. You can't change your mind halfway through, you can't double your rates and offer the same crappy level of service, you can't claim to be the best at what you do but not be able to back it up.

That said, I also know that it works. If you are prepared to do everything I've suggested in this book, you can and will totally transform your business. It will be a wild ride, there will be moments of doubt (lots of them, I'm guessing), and the urge to keep going back to being cheap or selling on price – but if you hold your ground and stick to the advice I've offered, follow the process and commit fully to being the absolute best at what you do, the rewards are stupendous.

It's about finding your own worth

I'm writing this closing chapter from a beach house that I've rented at the northern tip of Flinders Island in Tasmania. It's remote and isolated. I'm by myself. I've purposely come here to finish writing this book and to reflect on my life to this point.

This is my 35th year in business. I've written many books, they have been sold in over 65 countries and translated into every language from Nigerian to Russian. I've presented in over 25 countries around the world for over 500 companies. I've worked with thousands of business owners, presented to millions. I've helped over 700 people to write their first books, and many more to take their first steps on stage as speakers. I've been an Ambassador for charities and not-for-profits that matter to me, and I've been able to work with some pretty astonishing people – from Richard Branson to Tim Ferriss and many, many more. All of this came after I started life as an orphan, abandoned by my parents when I was six months old. The first 18 years of my life I struggled to find my value and to simply survive. Somewhere in there I found my worth.

This concept of charging what you are worth is actually much bigger than many of us realise. Taking it one step further, becoming the absolute best at what you do and by association being the most expensive, changed my life and enabled me to have a truly extraordinary life, one that I hope has much more to come. With learning my value to others, I discovered my own self-worth. And that has been transformational in every way. I realised a long time ago, just after 9/11, when I saw some graffiti on a subway wall in New York City, that said 'self-worth is more important than net worth'.

How wonderful if we can have both?

Where to from here?

Well, you made it. We covered a lot of ground and it seems like such a long time ago that I started by sharing my views on the world and the issue of small business poverty mentality. I hope I have been compelling enough to really convince you that this is a powerful strategy that has many rewards, but it won't come easily.

If what I spoke about resonated with you and really hit a few buttons that sparked an overwhelming desire to sit up and take notice, now the challenge is to take action. There is a process to follow, but it won't really work if you don't get your state of mind right and your overall strategy right. After all, if you've lived with a poverty mentality for a long time, as I did, it's not going to change overnight with a few positive affirmations and a chant. Get the conversation right in your head and the process will flow much more smoothly.

The big thing is knowing what to look forward to. As I type these final words, we are just coming to terms with a new world in the ongoing aftermath of COVID-19. I know that so many businesses were heavily impacted by this virus, let alone the human cost of course. But I'm pretty certain those businesses that have adopted a 'someone has to be the most expensive, why not make it you?' approach, are without a doubt, more likely to be the ones who have survived and possibly thrived.

Why? Because they were in better shape financially before the crisis started. Their customers were in better shape before the crisis started. These businesses could adapt quickly and still offer a quality product or service because they were robust and resilient and they knew how to stay relevant to their customers however they could.

The first businesses to fall were the price-driven ones, those who had no fat, no reserves, tight profit margins, poor service, poor online presence or online sales potential. And many of these were big businesses. This is not a size thing in the slightest. It's a state of mind thing.

I hope you make the transition, as a minimum to start charging what you are worth. And, if you are brave enough and capable enough, to becoming the most expensive by being the absolute best at what you do. Please share your stories with me – your trials and tribulations. And most importantly, stay true to the path once you begin. You can email me at hello@andrewgriffiths.com.au – I'd really love to hear from you.

My greatest desire is that you build the business you truly deserve. One that rewards you accordingly in every way. Where you get to do what you love and what you do best. Where your customers find you because of your reputation. Where you enjoy incredible loyalty from your customers, who encourage you to pursue your passion. And one where every single day, you get to experience the freedom that this kind of business truly offers.

'Man without a smiling face
should never open a shop.'
Chinese proverb

PLEASE SHARE YOUR STORIES AND EXPERIENCES

Now you know my strategy and my philosophy towards charging what you are worth. If you embrace this concept and make your new strategy, I'd love you to share how this has worked for you. What changed in your business? What changed in your life? Share your story with me.

I'd also be grateful if you can let me know about any businesses, anywhere on the planet, that you encounter who truly live up to the concept of 'Someone has to be the most expensive, why not make it you? But if you *are* going to be the most expensive, you also have to be the best'. I'm building a database of these businesses to illustrate the ideas I've put forward in this book.

Please email me at hello@andrewgriffiths.com.au.

About the author

Andrew Griffiths is a unique human being. Starting out as an orphan in Melbourne certainly set the scene for an unusual and in many ways extraordinary life. Today he is most known around the world for being a successful author and a powerfully inspiring speaker. He has a wisdom for business and for life in general, that gives his readers and his audiences the desire and the confidence to become more, in whatever way that matters to them.

Andrew's first career was as a Commercial Diver. His fascination with all things marine led him down this path and he purchased his first business at the age of 18. As he often says, buying a dive shop 30km from the ocean should have set alarm bells ringing about his business acumen. But like most origin stories, this, combined with a hard early life, created the greatest of learning experiences with many of his fundamental beliefs stemming from this stage of his life.

Of course like most of us, Andrew has had a number of careers and jobs. He worked in the exploration industry in Western Australia teaching survival skills and first aid to remote workers among other tasks. He has taught diving, run his own travel business, built and sold an outdoor advertising operation and had his own marketing company. He also worked for a large Japanese shipping company in the role of sales and marketing for one of their offshoot cruise companies. This saw him travelling the world, promoting and selling both the services of this company and the wonders of the Great Barrier Reef over a five-year span.

Andrew started writing books in 1999. Initially written to help small business owners overcome the common challenges they face, he has grown dramatically as an author. He was first published by well-known publisher Allen & Unwin in 2000, with the pivotal book, *101 Ways to Market Your Business*. The success of this book and the demand for it internationally led to him publishing a further 11 books with Allen & Unwin. He also published his first personal growth book, *The Me Myth*, with global publisher Simon & Schuster. Andrew has now written and published 14 books, sold in over 65 countries and translated into languages as diverse as Nigerian, Russian, Chinese, Vietnamese and Indian.

After living in Cairns, Far North Queensland for 30 years, Andrew recently moved to Melbourne, where he continues to write, to commentate on the world of business and to speak for organisations in Australia and around the planet. He has worked with hundreds of organisations globally including CBS, Hewlett Packard, the European Union, major banks, and telecommunication and media companies. Any organisation that has a lot of small business customers generally gets Andrew involved at some stage to inspire them, teach them and to help them build stronger businesses.

Of course Andrew still works with many small businesses through his various programmes and coaching, all aimed around strengthening small businesses in Australia and internationally. His wisdom and practical advice is always highly sought after and it's no surprise his nickname is *The Godfather of Small Business*.

After all is said and done though, Andrew's great love is for the natural world. He has a never ending supply of hilarious stories relating to wonderful experiences with weird and wonderful animals, on the land and in the oceans. The one thing that everyone who meets Andrew notices, is his giant heart. He truly is a remarkable and unique human being.

WANT SOME MORE ANDREW GRIFFITHS IN YOUR LIFE?

If you've got great value out of Andrew's latest book, there are a number of ways you can work with him. Check out the information on the following pages or visit his website at www.andrewgriffiths.com.au. And of course you can follow him on Facebook, LinkedIn and Instagram.

IF YOU LOVED THIS BOOK AS MUCH AS WE THINK YOU DID, WHY NOT SIGN UP FOR ANDREW'S NEW PROGRAMME?

SOMEONE HAS TO BE THE **MOST** EXPENSIVE WHY NOT MAKE IT YOU? **PROGRAMME**

This is an intensive and inspiring programme, designed to actually help business owners make the transition to either charging what they are actually worth or even better, becoming the most expensive and all that this entails.

Andrew's programme is all about transferring skills and knowledge in a practical way that empowers you to make the changes required. He teaches, coaches and helps to transform - with his very own unique style and approach. It's as much about mindset as it is about skill set.

If you'd like to know more about doing his programme individually or as part of a group, please drop us a line at info@andrewgriffiths.com.au.

THE MOST INSPIRATIONAL, PRACTICAL AND VALUABLE SMALL BUSINESS PROGRAMME EVER.

The AG BIZ CLUB has been a project on Andrew's drawing board for some time. As he travelled around the world, meeting and working with business owners from every corner of the planet, he had the growing realisation that the world of small business has become complex and complicated.

Andrew has been trying to find answers to all of this through his books, his writing and his speaking, but he wanted something more, something that was totally inclusive, where he could share his knowledge, experience and the learnings from what he was working on right now, as well as his 35 years of experience, with a group of small business owners in a truly powerful way. That's what the AG BIZ CLUB is all about.

Today overwhelm is an issue, overworking is an issue, lack of profit is an issue, keeping up with technology is an issue and business isolation is an issue. Small business owners need smart advice, practical knowledge, contemporary thinking and serious support to succeed today and that's exactly where the AG BIZ CLUB becomes an incredibly valuable resource for small business owners everywhere.

Check out the AG BIZ CLUB at www.andrewgriffiths.com.au. It's impressive and the perfect place for people of substance to build businesses of substance.

NOT ALL BUSINESS COACHES
ARE CREATED EQUAL?

There is no doubt that doing business has become increasingly challenging in recent years. The skills we used to find invaluable seem to have little place in the modern world. In the words of Alvin Toffler, author of the book *Futureshock*, "the illiterate of the twenty-first century will not be those who cannot read and write, but those who cannot learn, unlearn, and relearn". This is where we find ourselves today.

Andrew works with a limited number of business owners and entrepreneurs to help them build the business they really want and the business they deserve. In his own words, Andrew "works with people of substance to build businesses of substance".

The bottom line is that Andrew helps develop skills within your business and your team that will ensure you not only survive in the modern business world, but actually thrive. It's not about hustling, mindless scaling or treating customers like sheep. The one message that you would have taken away very clearly from this book is the concept of being the best. And Andrew's drive is to help you become exactly that.

If you'd like to find out more about working with Andrew please email info@andrewgriffiths.com.au.

www.andrewgriffiths.com.au

NEED A DYNAMIC, HIGHLY EXPERIENCED WORLD-CLASS SPEAKER FOR YOUR LIVE OR VIRTUAL EVENT?

Andrew Griffiths has delivered thousands of keynote presentations, workshops, webinars, programmes, seminars and retreats in over 25 countries. He has shared his entrepreneurial wisdom from America to Iran, from Japan to England, and his messages, like his books, are equally relevant in every market.

Andrew is an extremely capable speaker and a masterful storyteller. He leaves his audiences inspired, challenged and ready to take action. Andrew is able to draw as much on his own 35 year track record as a successful business owner, as his current global work as an Entrepreneurial Futurist. He is across the latest trends and the evolution of businesses in every corner of the planet.

Last but not least, Andrew has a down-to-earth style, one filled with great humour and humility, where his desire to help others shines through. Andrew is voted the "BEST SPEAKER" at events, time and time again, and his commitment is always to exceed everyone's expectations, something he unashamedly manages to do.

To find out more about getting Andrew to speak at your next event, either face to face or virtually – email info@andrewgriffiths.com.au.

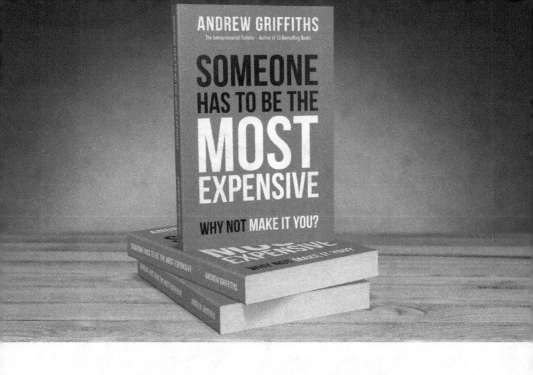

ARE YOU LOOKING FOR THE PERFECT GIFT FOR YOUR SMALL BUSINESS CUSTOMERS?

Over the last 20 years, Andrew's bestselling books have been sold in over 65 countries. They have been translated into languages as broad and diverse as Nigerian and Russian. There is no doubt that his messages and advice have great meaning, relevance and value to business owners and entrepreneurs globally.

Andrew's books are often bought in bulk where they are used as relationship-building tools, simple thank-you gifts, part of promotional campaigns and incentives and event gifts. One New Zealand based company purchased 10,000 copies of one book to give to every single small business customer of theirs in New Zealand and Australia.

If you are looking for the ideal gift for your business customers, Andrew's latest book is one of the most valuable presents you could possibly purchase. There are all kinds of ways to value add bulk book purchases, from special print runs with your company message printed in the book right through to having your own company message included as an introduction.

If this sounds like the ideal promotional opportunity for your organisation please email Andrew's team at info@andrewgriffiths.com.au.

WOULD YOU LIKE TO INTERVIEW ANDREW GRIFFITHS?

Over the last 20 years Andrew has been interviewed many times, across all types of media, in Australia and internationally. He is very comfortable being interviewed live on television and radio, as much as being interviewed for a feature in a publication or to appear on a podcast show.

Andrew can talk with great authority on the following:

- The evolution and future of business.
- The impact of COVID–19 on business locally and globally.
- Future-proofing business.
- Moving from transactions to experiences.
- Overcoming adversity and building resilience.
- The changing art of communication.
- Personal branding.
- All things small business.

If you would like to interview Andrew about any of the above or his latest book, *Someone Has To Be The Most Expensive, Why Not Make It You?*, please email info@andrewgriffiths.com.au.

Printed in the USA
CPSIA information can be obtained
at www.ICGtesting.com
LVHW041255151023
761121LV00001BB/131